I'd Rather Be Birding

A WARDLAW BOOK

I'd Rather Be Birding

JUNE OSBORNE

Foreword by Pete Dunne

TEXAS A&M UNIVERSITY PRESS   COLLEGE STATION

Most of the essays in this
book have been published
in different form in the
Waco Tribune-Herold, WildBird
magazine, and *Bird Watchers Digest*.

The paper used in this book
meets the minimum requirements
of the American National Standard for Permanence
of Paper for Printed Library Materials, z39.48-1984.
Binding materials have been chosen for durability.

Library of Congress Cataloging-in-Publication Data

Osborne, June, 1931–
    I'd rather be birding / June Osborne ; foreword by
Pete Dunne.—1st ed.
        p. cm.—(A Wardlaw book)
    ISBN 1-58544-292-5 (cloth : alk. paper)
    1. Bird watching.   2. Bird watching—Texas.
    3. Osborne, June, 1931–   I. Title.   II. Series.
    QL677.5.082   2003
    598'.07'234—dc21   2003012959

Dedication

My mind swirls when I think of the hundreds of people with whom I have shared the beauty and wonder of nature, especially birds, in the Texas Hill Country and other lovely places where I have been privileged to lead people to see their most-wanted birds.

You and all those who ever followed me and learned with me in bird identification classes, birding tours, and Elderhostels, all those I have met and talked to along uncounted birding trails, and everyone who has ever read a single word I have written—it is for you that I have lovingly prepared this book. ❧

CONTENTS

Exploring the Backyard

Travel Is for the Birds

In Love with a River

FOREWORD

Stop. What do you think you're doing? This is just a foreword, not the lead essay in *I'd Rather Be Birding,* and I'm just the guy they asked to warm up the readers before they move on to the main event (which is, of course, the writing of June Osborne).

If you know her writing, then you know you are in for a treat. If you are not yet a fan of one of birding's most effective wordsmiths, the treat will only be enhanced by the delight of discovery.

Seriously. Take my advice. Skip this foreword. Lick a finger. Start flipping pages. Get lost in the words that recreate a world of fun and excitement wrapped in feathers that millions of practitioners call birding and June Osborne describes so well.

Stubborn aren't you? OK, if you insist on seeing where this is going, I might as well scribe something worth your time and mine (even if what I have to say isn't a patch on the scope and quality of essays that lie ahead).

So just what is it about bird watching that is so all-fired captivating? Why is this avocation the fastest growing outdoor activity in North America and (measured in terms of overall popularity) second only to gardening as America's favorite outdoor pastime?

I get asked this question all the time (usually by reporters and 13- to 17-year-old nieces and nephews), and for the record I don't think I've ever formulated a satisfactory reply. But if you put my back to the wall, what I think lies at the heart of birding's popularity is that the endeavor is not a single pursuit, but many. "Birding," as the late Roger Tory Peterson was so fond of explaining, "can be so many things." While the subject is birds, the ambitions that propel people into the avocation are many and varied.

Take beauty. Most people take pleasure in beautiful objects. We see a Monet and it delights the eyes. We watch a morning sunrise and we smile.

Well, hue for hue, few elements in the mosaic of living things can match the colors and patterns of birds. If a sunrise makes us smile, a male cardinal at the window feeder makes optic nerves sizzle and the color appreciation centers of the brain go nova.

If you think Monet had a great sense of color and light, wait till you see a migratory fallout on the Gulf Coast. Dabs of paint, even inspired dabs of paint, can't approach the colors and vibrancy of hundreds of warblers, tanagers, and orioles all moving like multicolored sparks through the trees.

How about challenge? Our species seems to thrive on challenge. Birding can be as challenging a pursuit as it is gratifying. Back to the art theme. You go to an art museum. You expect to see great art, and you do. But paintings are predictable. They sit still. They don't hide. And unless part of the collection has been rotated into storage, paintings are pretty much always in the same place.

Birds are different. Birds are animate. They challenge us to find them. Challenge us to get a satisfactory look. They really up the ante. They demand (Rumpelstiltskin fashion) that we assign to them a name—and this is yet another reason why birding is so appealing. Birding has an intellectual side.

Oh, sure, some birds are easy to identify. Big and black and "caw, caw, caw" spells crow. If it looks like a duck, swims like a duck, and quacks like a duck it's a . . .

Well, maybe not. Loons look a lot like ducks (Red-throated Loon, an arctic breeder that winters along both seacoasts, even quacks!). And even if it is a duck, what kind of duck? Puddle duck or diving duck? You want a challenge? Try your skill (and luck) at identifying scaup. There's a challenge for you. And here's a story to illustrate it.

It happened at last year's World Series of Birding—a competition held in New Jersey every May in which teams of top field birders compete to see who can locate the most species of birds in 24 hours. Why would they do this? I told you. Because our species enjoys the challenge (and the fact that the event raises over half a million dollars for bird conservation is just a coincidence). Anyway, there was this scaup. Adult male. Perfectly close; perfectly visible. The top three teams (comprising of some of the finest birders in North America) studied the bird. Two of the teams called it Greater Scaup. One team identified it as Lesser Scaup. Bear in mind, only one of these identifications can be correct.

This story touches upon yet two more reasons why birding is so appealing. First, it never gets boring. Never. No matter how accomplished a birder you become, the horizon never gets closer. There is always a bird just a little too far, or a glimpse just a little too brief, or an identification just a little too subtle for your skill level to accommodate, *today.* Tomorrow may be different. Tomorrow your skills may have expanded to meet the challenge presented to you by that dirty, rotten, little feathered miscreant that bested you yesterday. You pin the correct name to the bird and win!

But the horizon is no closer. You take a step forward, the horizon takes a step back. Challenge, like gratification, is always a birder's companion in the field.

And the other point raised by the trial by scaup? It relates to misidentification, to failure. It's no big deal. Happens all the time. No birder or incipient birder should ever be anxious or afraid of tackling an identification challenge and being bested. Remember, the difference between an experienced birder and an inexperienced birder is that inexperienced birders have misidentified relatively few birds (so far). Experienced birders have misidentified thousands.

For all its challenge, birding is a low stakes game. A misidentification isn't fatal. It doesn't cause currencies to collapse or nations to fall. It doesn't precipitate famine. The equilibrium of the universe remains unaltered. Inexperience (and the fear of "looking dumb") should never prevent anyone calling their local nature center and signing on for the near mandatory bird walk or the regularly scheduled "Introduction to Birding" course.

Which brings up just one more reason that birding is so appealing. It's highly social! There are clubs. There are organizations. There are web sites, chat rooms, magazines that serve the communication needs of birders and . . .

There are columns. Like the one June Osborne writes for *WildBird* magazine; like the one she wrote for many years for the *Waco Tribune-Herald.*

I don't know how many nature columnists there are in North America. They serve a vast constituency. They help to keep the birding community informed. They serve to transform the would-be birders into enthusiastic birders. They have, to a man, woman, and scribe, my deepest respect. But within these august ranks, there are few June Osbornes. I've known her writing for years. I count myself one of her biggest fans. Here's why.

To the world's betterment, there are columnists who serve as a bridge between our species and the natural world. At one time an intimacy with nature was something Americans took for granted. Today, in the environmentally estranged atmosphere that characterizes urban and suburban existence, nature is something foreign. Columnists bridge the gap, making nature more understandable; making nature real.

June Osborne is such a columnist. Many of the essays found in this book are, at their core, instructional, even (dare I say it?) educational. They answer questions. They invite inquiry. They open eyes to wonders all around. But do not for a moment think that because they impart information, they must therefore be dull. Oh, no. There are columnists and there are columnists. One of the things that distinguishes skilled writers from mere writers (and one of the things that distinguishes June Osborne in particular) is the way they engage their readers. Skilled writing presupposes that the writer knows the subject (and few know birding better than June Osborne). But skilled writing also demands that the writer clearly define the objective and then have the communication skills to ferry the reader there.

My advice to you is to stop reading this foreword. Sit back. Start enjoying June Osborne's well-articulated ride into a world of challenge and discovery.

But, if in deference to writers of forewords, you have chosen to read this to the end, then let me add just one more insight, one thing that I think distinguishes June Osborne's writing from the pack.

You see, it's one thing to be knowledgeable. It's another thing to be verbally adroit. But it's quite another thing to be enthused (and for some odd reason many writers seem reluctant to let their enthusiasm show). While birding can be many things to many people, at its very core the study and appreciation of birds is supposed to be . . .

FUN! All caps. Fun to do; fun to read about.

So get to it. Get on to a collection of essays that describe, define, and affirm birding.

Thank you for your indulgence. It's been my pleasure to engage you for a time and to offer a great writer her due. But now it's time for me (and you) to get on to the important task of savoring *I'd Rather Be Birding*. The kudos go to June. But the pleasure will be yours and mine.

—Pete Dunne,
New Jersey Audubon's Cape May Bird Observatory

ACKNOWLEDGMENTS

I suppose you could say I started writing this book in the fall of 1980, for that is when my first published article appeared in Baylor University's alumni magazine, *The Baylor Line.* When I first saw my byline in print, a sleeping giant awoke within me and I knew that I must write. So, my sincere thanks go to Sherry Castello, then editor of the magazine, for giving me the push I needed to get started. Next, I wish to thank William H. Thompson, founding publisher of *Bird Watcher's Digest,* who sent me my first "rejection letter" when I submitted the same article to his delightful magazine. In it, he encouraged me to continue writing and invited me to submit another piece to him at a later date, which I did. It was accepted. So began an enjoyable relationship with *BWD.* Then I discovered a new kid on the block, *WildBird,* a magazine for which I wrote many articles during the 1980s. I thank Tim Gallagher and Bob Carpenter for those opportunities.

I took a hiatus from writing during the late 1980s to teach bird identification courses, lead birding tours, and teach in birding Elderhostels. In April, 1990, I received a letter from Shannon Davies, then a sponsoring editor at University of Texas Press, telling me that Ed Kutac, a birder extraordinaire from Austin, had suggested me as a possible author for a book on the Northern Cardinal. My heartfelt gratitude goes to Ed, from whom I learn something new about birds every time we converse and through whom my long association with Shannon began. A few years later, Shannon asked me to write a book on the Ruby-throated Hummingbird, which almost did not see the light of day because of family health crises during 1995–98, some of which were life threatening. Nevertheless, Shannon's patience and encouragement finally brought the book to the public in the fall of 1998.

Meanwhile, I wrote bird columns for the *Waco Citizen,* a weekly newspaper for which my son Sam was editor a short time. Thanks to Sam, my column titled "Wingin' It" was born. When Sam left the *Citizen,* I wrote from 1995 to 1997 for Paul Gately's weekly newsmagazine *The Radio Post,* published in Gatesville, Texas. Later, the editors of *WildBird* contacted me again and asked if I would be interested in writing for them on a regular basis, at the same time inviting me to serve on their advisory board. June Kikuchi, Amy Hooper, and Roger Sipe at *WildBird* are a fun bunch with whom to work. In November, 1998, Barbara Elmore, then managing editor of the *Waco Tribune-Herald,* invited me to write "Wingin' It" on alternate Saturdays for my hometown. From that time until February 2003 I worked with several editors at the *Trib.* I owe a tremendous debt of gratitude to all the readers who have encouraged me to continue writing all these years through their kind words in response to my articles and columns.

The book you now hold is a collection of my work from these many venues, beginning in 1980. A version of almost every essay in the book was first printed in one of these publications.

Putting together a collection such as this requires teamwork from a number of people. The entire staff at Texas A&M University Press has enthusiastically supported this project from the beginning. Without them the book would not exist. I thank them one and all.

Copyeditor Dale Wilson made the book better than it would have been without his careful reading and correcting of the manuscript.

From the start I hoped to get Pete Dunne to write the foreword. It was a happy day, indeed, when he agreed to do so. Pete, I owe you one.

Janet Sheets, reference librarian at Baylor University's Moody Library, never ceases to amaze me when I ask for information on whatever species I happen to be writing about. An avid birder herself, Janet has a knack for finding stacks and stacks of articles from scientific journals as well as the popular literature.

Sharlande Sledge, whose name you will read in many of my essays, is not only a devoted friend and birding companion but also an impeccable proofreader/editor/ex–English teacher whose comments and red marks I trust and heed. She can spot misplaced commas and quotation marks quicker than I can spot a Vermilion Flycatcher in plain sight.

Barbara Garland contributed her beautiful photography to illustrate many of my earlier articles and all the photos for my book *The Cardinal.* She and I had many fun birding trips together while seeking all the right birds for her to photograph. You will meet her through some of my birding adventures told about in this book.

I thank Father Tom Pincelli and Beth Kingsley Hawkins for their evaluations of the original manuscript. Their perceptive comments and suggestions were taken to heart.

I gratefully acknowledge my long association with the owners and staff at Neal's Lodges in Concan, Texas. They have become my extended family, and I love each and every one of them. It would take a whole page to list all of their names, but Mary Anna and Rodger Roosa and Carol and Johnny Graves would top the list. My love for the area around their lodge has colored the way I look at life and, consequently, the way I write.

My three sons—Mike, Van, and Sam, who have been behind me all the way—contributed their delightful art to illustrate this work. The reason you see Sam's name in my stories more often than the other two is because the older chicks had flown the nest by the time I became addicted to birding and so did not get to go on as many birding trips with me as their younger brother.

My husband Harold, a retired sociology professor, has shown infinite patience with a wife who always seems to be at the computer with a deadline to meet. He has literally held my hand and helped me over many a rough place throughout my birding and writing career. He is my best and most honest critic and I accept his red marks and suggestions with gratitude. He gave his undying support even when I was gone from home for weeks at a time on birding excursions. He graciously granted permission for three of his poems—"The Owl," "The Chickadee," and "The Nest"—to be included in this collection.

Last, but not least, there is Shannon Davies: my friend, supporter, adviser, confidante, cheerleader, and editor. How can I ever thank her enough for the joys of writing she has brought into my life? As Shannon and I often say, "Don't you just love to have written?"

INTRODUCTION

In *Pilgrim at Tinker Creek,* Annie Dillard wrote: "Beauty and grace are performed whether or not we *will* or *sense* them. The least we can do is try to be there." Dillard's words became my creed when I began my quest for birds in 1975. I took a bird identification course at McLennan Community College taught by my mentor, Jean Schwetman. The spring field trips were in "The Pecan Bottoms" in Waco's Cameron Park. Then and there, I discovered warblers that were passing through in migration, fairly dripping from the pecan trees. Before taking Jean's course I had no idea such colorful birds existed, much less that I could see some of them in my own Waco, Texas, backyard. After this epiphany in Cameron Park I became addicted to the sport of bird watching and soon began traveling to see birds. As Dillard suggested, I wanted to *be there* for as many of nature's performances as possible.

From the beginning, my passion for birds was so strong that I read everything about them I could get my hands on. By 1980 I was so obsessed with my new knowledge that I gathered the young children in my neighborhood and took them on bird walks in *their* own backyards. Then I branched out to teaching senior citizens through our city's Parks and Recreation Department. I began writing about birds that same year. The next year, I started teaching bird identification courses through Baylor University's continuing education division, a job that snowballed into leading birding tours in Texas, Arizona, Florida, Louisiana, Arkansas, Mexico, and Central America.

In 1985 I discovered Concan (not Cancun), eighty miles west of San Antonio in the Texas Hill Country at the southern edge of the Edwards Plateau. It all started with an article about Neal's Lodges in the magazine *Texas Highways.* A neighbor, Louise McCollum, who is also a birder, read the article, and she and her husband Bob went for a visit. When they got home they told me there was a place I had to go, where Hooded Orioles came to the sugar-water feeder right outside their cabin door and Vermilion Flycatchers hung out near the river. A few months later I drove to Concan to see for myself. The moment I laid eyes on the Frio River it was love at first sight. I took my first group of birders to Neal's Lodges in 1986 and have been at it ever since.

When I became involved in Baylor University's Elderhostel program, I conducted the classes at Neal's. I have lost count of the number of birding Elderhostels I held there over the years, and I certainly have no idea how many people attended them; but I can tell you that every April, when I am at Neal's as the resident birder, numerous former Elderhostelers come by to see me when they are birding in Texas. The first time they went to Neal's, they, too, fell in love with the place and the river, and they return every chance they get.

Once you begin your quest for nature, you will never, ever have an excuse to be bored again in your whole life. You can't possibly watch birds without noticing butterflies or grasses or wildflowers or trees or mushrooms. You can't go owling or to the Frio Bat Cave without looking at the stars and planets and constellations and fireflies. It is all connected. Around a curve in the road you will spot a patch of lavender foxglove that others may have missed. For the same amount of money you would spend on a Saturday night movie, you can see millions of Mexican Free-tailed Bats. For no price except your attention, you may notice that the knot on the end of a branch isn't a knot at all, but a Black-chinned Hummingbird's nest. And you can see hundreds of fireflies lighting up the early night sky on a hayride by the river absolutely free.

I love "the ripple effect." I often think of an old Baptist Sunday School motto, "Each one, teach one." Everyone can make a difference. The passion for nature watching is contagious. One person catches it and passes it on to another, then that one passes it to another, and the ripples keep going and going and going like the pink rabbit on TV that runs on Energizer batteries.

So the ripples continue. World-traveling birders tell me they planned just to pass *through* Concan on their way to the Rio Grande Valley or Big Bend or High Island, but once they arrive and see what is there, they wish they had planned to stay longer. And so, I have put together this collection of my work for you, which, in reality, is a collection of memories gathered in my own backyard, in the backyards of the world, and in my special place, Concan, Texas. You can tell from the accounts of these living memories that of all the activities that enrich my life, really, *I'd rather be birding.*

Exploring

the Backyard

Hey, Mom!

Crouching behind a thorny bush
at the top of a wooded culvert not far from my home,
I waited for the avian show to begin.

A Song Sparrow flitted into the creek,
splashed water over its back, then flew out of sight.
A shocking burst of lemon-yellow in a treetop close by
signaled the presence of a Yellow-rumped Warbler.
Again and again he flew out and back from his perch over-
    head,
acting like a flycatcher in his quest for tiny insects on the
    wing.

A flock of Red-winged Blackbirds gurgled "konk-la-reee" in
    a distant field.
Turkey Vultures and Red-tailed Hawks made lazy ovals in
    the sky,
gliding on the warm thermals of midday above the river.

Other woodland sights and sounds invaded my reverie.
Somewhere in the woods a Northern Cardinal called to
    his mate.
A Great Blue Heron, startled by an unknown presence,
    spread its wings, almost as wide as the river, and silently
    stole away.
A spirited Carolina Chickadee gaily sang its sprightly song
    while a flock of Blue Jays exchanged boisterous greetings.

Suddenly, a sound like potato wagons bumping along a
　country road abruptly woke me from my musing, and I
　knew I must go.
Fierce, boiling storm clouds were approaching from the west.

A hundred yards downstream a man and a young boy
　strolled leisurely along the rocky margin of the river.
With eyes downcast they scanned every stone in search of
　fossils,
totally unaware of any activity beyond their own.
As I descended from my lofty vantage point and started
　toward them,
the boy looked up from his intensive hunt.
"Hey, Mom!" he yelled. "Did you see any birds?" ❧

Diamonds in Your Own Backyard

I got hooked on birds during spring migration in 1975 and soon learned four things: birding is addictive, highly contagious, easily transmitted, and if you want to see an abundance of exotic birds you must be willing to travel beyond your own backyard. Soon after I got the "bug," my husband, Harold, and youngest son, Sam, were infected. I hooked them by making birds a major emphasis on family outings—beginning with picnics in the park and Sunday afternoon drives to Lake Waco. After that it was easy to convince them that seeing birds while traveling away from home would add a dimension to our lives none of us had dreamed possible.

Soon thereafter, no longer did we choose a vacation destination simply for its scenic or historical value. Rather, we chose the birding hot spots of the nation (and later of the world), using "target" birds as our guide in decisions on where to go. Thumbing through bird guides, we picked out species we wanted to see and planned trips to the most likely locations to see them. This turned out to be a good way to have unforgettable family adventures.

For our first real birding vacation, we chose as our most-wanted bird the Brown-capped Rosy-Finch, which has a limited range in the central Rockies. Thus, Colorado was the place to go. Along with our birding companions, Bill and Cozy Adams and their son David, we made reservations for two cabins at the YMCA of the Rockies near Estes Park. As is my custom, shortly after our arrival I set out food and water for the birds that might come to the front porch of our cabin. Soon we had Steller's Jays, White-breasted and Pygmy Nuthatches, Black-billed Magpies, Common Ravens, and others coming to the feast.

All these birds were wonderful, but we really wanted to see our "target bird," the Brown-capped Rosy-Finch. We asked the park naturalist where we were most likely to see the birds at that time of year. She told us we were almost guaranteed to find them on the trail to Cub Lake. We picked up a trail map, and the six of us piled into the car and set out to find the trailhead.

Studying the map very quickly, we decided this expedition should take no longer than forty-five minutes to an hour. At the time, Sam was four years old, David about ten. I'd had minor surgery two weeks before and was not exactly in tip-top shape for a mountainous hike. Nevertheless, we hit the trail with high expectations. Inexperienced hikers that we were, we made an almost fatal mistake at the very beginning. Thinking we would be on the trail no longer than an hour, we took no water or food except for a granola bar I had stashed in my pocket. We know better now.

An hour later, on a trail that was sometimes obscured by fallen trees and patches of ice, we had not seen a single bird, much less a rosy-finch. We weren't even sure we were still on Cub Lake Trail. After three hours Bill and Harold took turns carrying Sam on their shoulders, and five hours into the trail that seemed to lead us 'round and 'round the mountain, I begged them to leave me and let me die. At that point, the group voted and decided Sam and I should share the granola bar. Well, we finally stumbled onto Cub Lake, where we did something else dangerous. We dipped our hands into the clear water and drank. Dying of thirst or not, we would not dare do that today.

After hiking seven hours on this treacherous mountain trail, where we did not see a rosy-finch or anything else with feathers, we simply felt fortunate that we all survived to get back to the parking lot, the car, and our cabins.

The next morning I was awakened shortly after sunrise by a phone call from our friends next door. Bill casually said, "June, go look on your front porch." I looked through our picture window and was astounded to see a hundred or more Brown-capped Rosy-Finches gorging themselves on the sunflower seeds I had placed there the night before.

Remember that old fable about the man who traveled the world over in search of treasure, only to return home to find "acres of diamonds" in his own backyard? Well? ๑

A Case for Serendipity

Serendipity: "the faculty for making desirable discoveries by accident."
—The Random House Dictionary of the English Language

Two distinct styles of birding are "Extravaganza" and "Serendipity." Extravaganza's success requires careful planning and precise timing to produce myriad species of birds sighted at a single location or on a given day. Serendipity is the casual, undesigned type of birding that nets small, unexpected rewards. Its success depends wholly on the individual's being at the right place at the right time and surrendering to surprise. Both styles depend on the observer's being watchful.

Since I like surprises, serendipity is my favorite of the two styles. In more than a quarter of a century of birding I have experienced serendipity many times. One of the most memorable times was in 1978 when Harold, Sam, and I had an eye-to-eye encounter with a Bald Eagle. Driving down a remote New Mexico road, we were suddenly aware of a huge bird descending above us. As it swung low over our car for a roadside landing, we realized we were in the presence of our country's symbol. To our amazement, the majestic eagle perched on a wooden fence post, so close we didn't need binoculars.

Driving up Oregon's coast one summer, we behaved as most tourists do, stopping at every overlook to admire the mystical beauty of the area. At each stop we saw the same three people, a man and two women, scanning the misty coastline with binoculars. Obviously, they were birders like us. At our third mutual stop we spied a Tufted Puffin far out in the water. The puffin's appearance inspired spirited conversation among us and we made introductions all around. The comical-looking bird turned out to be a "Lifer" for all of us. Many birders keep what they call a Life List. The first time you see a certain bird, it goes down on your list as a Lifer.

Our three new friends from New Jersey arrived at the next stop a few minutes before we did. By the time we got there, they had their scope set up and focused on a colorful Harlequin Duck posing on a rock near the water's edge. The duck is named for a stock character of Italian comedy who wears a mask and parti-colored tights, a perfect description of the actor who played the role of our second Lifer in fifteen minutes.

On another occasion I visited Dan Brown's "Hummer Haven" in Christoval, Texas. Standing on a small dam on the Concho River, Dan and I were startled when a flock of forty-five birds lifted into the blue sky above the bend of the river. At first we thought they were Sandhill Cranes. When they were directly overhead, I knew without a doubt they were Black-crowned Night-Herons. They circled time and time again not far above the treetops. Dan had never seen them on his ranch before. When we looked down at the concrete on which we stood we caught on to why they were persistent in circling that particular area: Bird droppings were all over the place. We moved out quietly so the birds could return to their favorite resting place. Soon they landed on the concrete embankment, taking their places as if each knew where the other was supposed to be.

One afternoon, while collecting information for a roadrunner story at the country home of my friend Ann Cunningham, she and I were mesmerized by the birds at the feeders near her front porch. At first it was a constant parade of the usual: Carolina Chickadees, Tufted Titmice, Northern Cardinals, Ruby-throated Hummingbirds, and House Finches. Then, to our great delight, a small, short-tailed, acrobatic bird appeared, clinging upside down to the wire sunflower feeder. The animated Red-breasted Nuthatch was totally unexpected since nuthatches are not regular visitors to McLennan County in Central Texas. The nuthatch is an irruptive migrant, its winter range varying greatly from year to year. When they *do* appear, it is usually during a cold winter up north when their food is scarce and the birds move south in order to survive.

Same afternoon, same tree, a Black-and-white Warbler crept down the limb above the feeder. Ann and I found it amusing that two "upside-down birds" showed up only minutes apart. Both forage going headfirst down a limb or tree trunk. Ann had never seen either species in her yard.

On an early morning hike outside Red River, New Mexico, our family was following a clear mountain stream when Sam, our young spotter, suddenly called out, "There's a dipper!" At the far edge of the stream we saw a solitary wren-like bird with slate-gray plumage and short stocky build. I don't know who its choreographer is, but the American Dipper is quite a dancer, comically bobbing its way along over the slippery rocks. With strong legs and special oil glands, the dipper is able to keep its footing even when in water far over its head. In fact, the bird has the incredible ability to "fly" under as much as twenty feet of rushing water to reach feeding places at the bottom of a stream. Even though it has webless feet, it often tries to swim on the water's surface like a duck. We watched the dipper for thirty minutes as it rhythmically danced down the river, around a bend, and out of our sight.

Several years ago I was conducting a birding Elderhostel in the Texas Hill Country. Early one October morning, as we drove into the pecan bottoms at Park Chalk Bluff on the Nueces River, I saw something I had never seen before: Thousands of Monarch butterflies were awakening and lifting off from the trees like wispy orange clouds. They undoubtedly were on their way to their winter home west of Mexico City.

While attending an outdoor wedding at Lake Whitney near my hometown, serendipity played itself out at its finest. At the beginning of the ceremony one of the officiants announced that we would observe a moment of silence in remembrance of the groom's uncle, who died a few weeks before. As soon as the minister said the words "Uncle Pete," a Tufted Titmouse whistled its loud, unmistakable "Peter! Peter! Peter!" Again, when the minister mentioned the name "Uncle Pete," the titmouse's whistle rang true. At no other time during the ceremony did I hear the titmouse call, nor any other bird for that matter.

On a birding tour of southeastern Arizona, the oldest participant was eighty-three-year-old retired missionary Kitty Cooper. Kitty was a delight and kept up with the group remarkably well for her age. One day when we were at Santa Rita Lodge in Madera Canyon, she decided to stay in her cabin when I told her the group was going on a rather rugged mountain trail in search of an Elegant Trogon. We were gone for several hours, and though we tried our hardest, we never spotted the bird. When we returned to the lodge, Kitty told me that while we were gone she watched the birds in the creek below the windows at the back of her cabin. She described a bird she had seen bathing in the creek and preening on a large rock. She perfectly described the Elegant Trogon. Later that day Kitty asked me, "June, why do you suppose I got to see that bird and the rest of the group didn't?" I told her she just happened to be in the right place at the right time. Kitty was ninety-six at the time of this writing. Every time we see each other we enjoy recounting the day of her unforgettable serendipity.

One day I was walking through the kitchen when I saw a small black object on our white floor. At first I thought it was a sunflower seed, but when I stooped to pick it up I found something far more precious: It was a wee hummingbird feather, so tiny I was afraid my breath would blow it away and I'd never find it again. I got out my ten-power hand lens so I could examine it more closely and took it to a patch of sunlight. I could scarcely believe what I saw: In the diminutive object that I held in my hand was a microscopic piece of the rainbow—an overall wash of deep violet, with flecks of indigo, blue, and aquamarine iridescence added to the spectrum. I thought it just had to be a gorget feather from a male Black-chinned Hummingbird.

How did a hummingbird feather find its way to my kitchen floor? It must have been on the bottom of someone's shoe. But how did it get stuck to the sole of that someone's shoe? I don't know for sure, of course, but my theory is that a hummer slammed into the reflection on my storm door, knocked loose a throat feather or two, then flew on its way. My son Mike had just been in and out the front door, and the feather could have been on the porch when he came inside. All I know for sure is that shortly after Mike left I found one of the greatest gifts I have ever received: a perfect piece of God's handiwork, so small and lovely I cannot find the right adjectives to describe it—a small gift of wonder, straight from God's hand to mine. What serendipity! Now, I ask, what shape do angels take when they come to call?

Pishing or Spishing?

A simple method of attracting birds, other than providing food, water, and shelter, is called "pishing" by most birders. The American Birding Association (ABA) now calls it "spishing," but to me it sounds more like it begins with a "P." Purse your lips as if you're getting ready for a big kiss, then say, "Pssshhh! Pssshhh! Pssshhh!" repeatedly, until you run out of spit or breath, whichever comes first. The sound is supposed to simulate the cries of a baby bird in distress. It arouses the curiosity of the birds that hear it and they come to investigate.

One cool, cloudy day in January, I was walking near a wooded area on the street parallel to our street. All along I noticed a great deal of bird activity in the trees. Light rain fell intermittently all morning, and the birds were taking advantage of a lull between showers to grab a bite to eat. Cedar Waxwings by the hundreds were in the tops of hackberry trees, uttering that weird, high-pitched wheeze that is their only song. Yellow-rumped Warblers flitted about like flycatchers in search of waterlogged insects. American Goldfinches called out their orders for "po-ta-to-chips" while flying roller-coaster fashion between trees. Closer to the woods, I saw a Brown Creeper coming in for a landing at the base of a tree ten feet away. Brown Creepers are so camouflaged with cryptic, streaked brown plumage that it is almost impossible to see them against a tree trunk. The creeper proceeded in its methodical spiral up and around the tree's trunk in search of food before flying to another low landing nearby and repeating the exercise.

A male Northern Cardinal foraged for food in the underbrush. Had it not been for his brilliant red plumage shining through the brambles like a red light, I would have missed him. Ruby-crowned Kinglets and one Golden-crowned Kinglet came near as I peered into the woods.

A Hermit Thrush with dark spots on its breast and a rufous tail made a brief appearance, dropped low from its high perch, then disappeared down the ravine.

Out of curiosity I decided to "pish" to see what other species of birds might come out of hiding. I could hardly believe what happened next: ten Ruby-crowned Kinglets joined the golden-crown in a chorus of their fussy call notes. The crown patch of the golden-crown was erect, making him look shaggy-headed. One of the ruby-crowns came so close I thought he was going to climb into my pocket. They just *have* to be the most curious of birds!

Five Carolina Chickadees joined the chorus singing, "Chick-a-dee-dee-dee!" Then two Tufted Titmice added their "Peter! Peter! Peter!" One Cedar Waxwing examined the "Pisher" from a polite distance of twelve feet. I suppose the rest of the flock appointed him as their emissary. From somewhere I heard an American Crow calling raucously. I seriously doubt if he was responding to my "pishing."

The rest of the Cedar Waxwing crew maintained their distance across the street, but curiosity got the best of the goldfinches. Soon a dozen or so were clamoring overhead, telling me with their ascending call how "sweee-EEET" I am. They were probably some of the flock that gorge themselves at my feeders every day. They seemed to say: "Hey! We know you! You're the one who fills those funny containers with the delicious black stuff we love."

A Yellow-rumped Warbler added his soft "chink" to the percussion section of the chorus. An Orange-crowned Warbler appeared. This plain-looking grayish-olive bird with no distinctive markings made a loud "kissing" sound as it observed me, and several Dark-eyed Juncos surrounded me with their metallic clicking.

Under poor lighting conditions, sometimes you must rely on silhouette and behavior to make a correct identification. When the Hermit Thrush reappeared in the shadows, I knew immediately what it was, although all I could see were a dark silhouette, drooping wings, and a subtle flicking of its tail.

Other curiosity-seekers responding to my "pishing" were Carolina Wrens, tails cocked in the air; American Robins hopping across the lawn in search of worms; and a Downy Woodpecker with its "whinny" call. Finally, Inca Doves chimed in, proclaiming, "No hope!" In spite of their dismal warnings I kept having good luck with my "pishing" efforts.

I couldn't decide who was the more curious, the pish-ER or the pish-EES. In five minutes I "pished" up over a dozen different species of birds that I would not have seen had I not tried this simple method. All came within fifteen feet of the place where I stood.

Strolling back up the street to return home, I waved at familiar motorists passing by. I couldn't help thinking, "If only they knew the wonders that are just around the corner, they wouldn't be in such a hurry to get wherever it is they are going."

If you have the nerve to do something your neighbors would think was crazy if they could see and hear you doing it, I dare you to try this. On second thought, perhaps you should go to a secluded spot where no one can see you. "Pishing" or "spishing"—no matter what you call it, make sure the area you choose is a good bird habitat. As soon as you're set, purse your lips and repeatedly say, "Pssshhh! Pssshhh! Pssshhh!" Then count the birds that come to you. ৯

Name That Bird in Three Notes or Less

I was still in bed when I heard a loud, squawking, "Jay! Jay! Jay!" I knew the Blue Jay was scolding me because there were no peanuts in his bowl. Still trying to wake up enough to get out of bed, I heard "Caw! Caw! Caw!" It was a crow pleading for cracked corn. The Northern Cardinal's "Cheer! Cheer! Cheer!" brought me to full consciousness. The three of them seemed to be imploring me to "Get out of bed, you sleepyhead!"

I often "bird by ear" before getting up in the morning. Some birdsongs and calls are so familiar we don't even have to think about them when we hear them. We instantly recognize the call of a jay or a crow or a cardinal. But many songs are not so familiar and we must work to memorize them. When you hear an unfamiliar melody, try to track it down. Observing a bird in full song helps form a mental as well as audible image to file away in your memory bank.

When you think of the more than nine hundred species of birds in North America and their myriad songs, the task of trying to learn even a few seems daunting. Why not start with the birds in your own backyard and the night birds you hear after dark? If you have a good imagination, try putting words to their songs. American Goldfinches place their orders for "po-TAY-toe-CHIPS" as they fly in roller-coaster fashion above your head. Then, when they land at your feeder, they tell you how "swee-EET" you are. Robins greet the morning with "cheerily, cheer-up, cheerio" or "tut, tut, tut"—sounding for all the world as if they are laughing at you. Tufted Titmice yell "Peter! Peter! Peter!" Carolina Wrens utter a loud "tea-kettle, teakettle, teakettle." All wrens have powerful voices for such tiny birds.

Among woodpeckers, drumming replaces song. When you hear this distinct sound, you know it's a woodpecker, but which one? Hairy and Downy Woodpeckers are found across almost all the United States. The hairy's drumming is a very fast buzzing that slows toward the end. The notes are indistinguishable and fairly long, with long pauses between drums. The downy's drumming is so slow you can almost count the notes. Its call is a short, gentle, flat "pik" followed by a soft whinny that sounds like a pony. Hairy's call note is a sharp, strong "peek" that is louder and higher-pitched than downy's. Some birds sing their names. All species of chickadees sing some variation of "CHICK-a-dee-dee-dee." Northern Bobwhites definitely say "Bob-WHITE!" Eastern and Spotted Towhees call "tow-HEE!" or a loud "mew" and invite you to "drink-your-teeeeeeeee!" Eastern Phoebe tells you who it is with its distinctive "FEE-bee." The Killdeer calls out "kill-DEE! kill-DEE!" and the Eastern Wood-Pewee plaintively calls "PEE-oh-WEE." On summer nights listen for "Chuck-will's-widow" repeatedly announcing its name. Also at night, when you hear "Who-cooks-for-YOU? Who-cooks-for-YOU-awl?" rest assured it's a Barred Owl. A nasal "peent" indicates that a Common Nighthawk is searching for insects around yard lights.

I am trying to teach our two-year-old grandson Jack to recognize bird sounds. We have a Lefton China Great Horned Owl figurine on the living room coffee table. When Jack was still crawling I showed him the owl whenever he came for a visit. I hooted, "Who—whoo—who, who, who," trying to get him to imitate me. For the longest time Jack would not repeat the sound, but I could see his wheels turning. I knew he was storing the sound for future reference. Then one day, without prompting, he went straight to the coffee table, and said, "Who—whoo—who, who, who." Now, every time he sees the owl or a picture of an owl he makes the sound. Often when we baby-sit Jack, we watch his favorite videos over and over, *Tigger* and *Winnie-the-Pooh*. When he sees the character "Owl" he goes into his rendition of the Great Horned Owl. Once in a while I sneak in a tape of real birds and he sits enraptured throughout the entire video. When a colorful warbler or bunting flies onto the scene, Jack immediately calls out "bird-EE!" and "cheep, cheep." We're pretty sure we have a budding young birder-by-ear on our hands.

Learning birdsongs at any age is fun, challenging, and rewarding. Once you master a few songs and calls, you won't have to see a bird to know what is hiding in the treetops. Each bird's song is as unique as a fingerprint. Once you can name that bird in your backyard in three notes or less, you're ready to move on to the birds of the world. §➤

Birding by Chair

It was a balmy January morning in southern Arkansas. Harold and I were visiting his sister Alene and her husband, R. B. They live at the edge of Norphlet, a small town that makes it feel like you're "out in the country."

All morning I'd caught glimpses through the den windows of Brown Thrashers chasing each other and Northern Mockingbirds guarding their berry supplies. Through the kitchen window I saw a flock of black birds, repeatedly dropping from the tall trees to the ground and flying back up again. Without my binoculars I assumed they were grackles since grackles seem to be everywhere.

Knowing my addiction to birds, the other members of the family finally said, "June, why don't you go outside and see what you can see?" Skeptically, they added, "There's probably not much out there." That was all the challenge I needed. Hoping to prove them wrong, I took my binoculars and headed for the patio.

At the side of the house there's an open space covered with gravel where guests park their cars. When I stepped onto the patio and focused binoculars on the black birds, I discovered a mixed flock of Brewer's Blackbirds and Brown-headed Cowbirds gathering grit from the gravel to help digest their food. Male Brewer's Blackbirds are black all over throughout the year, with a purplish sheen on head and neck and a greenish gloss on the back. They have yellow eyes. At a distance they can easily be mistaken for Common Grackles. Female Brewer's are mostly brown with brown eyes. Male cowbirds have a brown head and a black body. Females are grayish brown all over. Most blackbirds travel in mixed flocks in the winter.

Having identified the flock, I turned my eyes to the backyard. No ordinary birder's backyard this. It has no sunflower feeders, no suet log, no wire cylinder filled with peanuts, no corn-on-the-cob for squirrels, no thistle (nyjer) feeder for goldfinches, and no birdbath—all the elements we think necessary to attract birds to an urban backyard. What Alene and R. B. have is perfect habitat suitable for a variety of birds with abundant wild food available.

Next to the house are two sycamore trees, a mulberry tree, and a wide-open space with a telephone wire stretching across its width. Behind that is a patch of small trees, shrubs, and weeds gone wild. Past that is another open space, a pond, and thick mixed woods of sycamore, sweet gum, oak, cypress, and pine trees—a veritable forest. This landscaping was by no means accomplished by design. It evolved naturally over several decades.

I pulled up a chair, sat down, and started "pishing." Again, a number of birds approached to investigate the sound. A Northern Mockingbird was first to respond to my maniacal sound. White flags in its tail and wings flashing, it flitted to the edge of the clearing. Then a pair of Northern Cardinals appeared, the male bright red against green shrubs. Hearing a clicking sound, I looked up and found a Yellow-rumped Warbler (the Myrtle race) in the tree next to the house. It had a white throat and bright yellow patches on its rump, sides, and top of its head.

A Red-shouldered Hawk soaring overhead called out its clear, high "kee-ah." A Blue Jay, at eye level, mocked the hawk, while an American Robin chortled its "tut, tut, tut."

Harold came outside and walked with me to the pond. There we heard "Old Sam Peabody, Peabody, Peabody," then saw the White-throated Sparrow that had uttered it. Chipping and Field Sparrows played at the pond's edge while American Goldfinches foraged in the treetops. No fancy thistle feeders for them, thank you very much. They were going after fluffy sycamore seed balls, their favorite food in the wild. On our way back to the house, three Eastern Bluebirds greeted us from the telephone wire. Before I reluctantly went inside for lunch, the last bird I saw, an Eastern Towhee, stayed just long enough to make it to my list of twenty species in one hour. Once we were back inside, the group asked dubiously, "Well?" to which I nonchalantly replied, "All ya gotta do is show up."

The older I get, the more I enjoy "birding by chair," sitting in one place, letting the birds come to me. Alene's backyard is a perfect place for such an activity. During a spring visit there that same year, on Saturday and Sunday mornings, while the siblings were retelling stories from their upbringing during the Great Depression, I slipped out to the backyard for some more easy birding, knowing full well the others would never even miss me. Placing my chair in the shade behind the house, I waited for the avian parade to begin.

Since ripe mulberries are natural magnets for fruit-eating birds, I sat near the mulberry tree for two hours each morning and saw a total of twenty-seven species without leaving my chair. In years long gone, the place where I sat was Alene's garden, which produced bushels of tomatoes, black-eyed peas, cucumbers, corn, onions, and strawberries for Alene's unsurpassable strawberry pie. This area is now a grassy lawn, a hedgerow delineating the back border. A few fruit trees—apple, pear, and peach—are randomly scattered around the grounds.

Since I see Brown Thrashers every time we go to Alene's, seeing one foraging in the hedgerow would not have surprised me. However, I was surprised to see five of them, which turned out to be a family of three offspring with their parents. The young, although equally as large as the adults, followed them around the yard with fluttering wings, like baby birds begging to be fed. Every few minutes one of them spread a wing and tilted its body toward the sun, soaking in some rays. Had I not known about sunbathing among birds, I would have thought they were sick or simply out of kilter. Instead, I marveled that birds so young already knew sunbathing techniques.

A male Orchard Oriole landed in the top of the mulberry tree, grabbed a berry, and flew away. Soon his mate did the same. A Northern Mockingbird flew repeatedly to the mulberry tree, then back to a leafy hideaway in the neighbor's poplar tree where there must have been a nest filled with hungry nestlings.

I heard the song of a distant Summer Tanager, which finally showed up in the mulberry tree. A Blue Jay with twigs in its beak flew across the yard. I wondered where it would build its nest. An Eastern Kingbird, Eastern Wood-Pewee, Yellow-billed Cuckoo, and Great Crested Flycatcher all made unexpected appearances. A skulking Gray Catbird made a beeline from the base of a Catawba to the mulberry tree.

In the distance I heard a Pileated Woodpecker's loud, distinctive "wuck, wuck, wuck." In Arkansas they call it "the Lord Gawd Bird" because it is so big and loud. A brilliant flash of red, white, and black drew my attention to a handsome Red-headed Woodpecker, especially welcome since I had not seen this species in years and certainly did not expect it to be a backyard bird.

When I went back in the house, the others, with the slightest hint of a snicker, casually asked, "Did you see any birds?" I answered just as casually, "Yeah, a few." They couldn't believe I had seen twenty-seven species. The secret is picking the right spot, sitting quietly, and waiting for the parade to begin. Having a mulberry tree loaded with succulent, ripe berries doesn't hurt. "Birding by Chair" proved to be a productive and enjoyable way for me to spend the mornings at Alene's house in the country.

The Muse

One May evening, my husband Harold, my friend Sharlande, and I came out of the shopping mall in time to see ominous clouds like swirls of dirty snow stretching from horizon to horizon. We looked for any sign of a twister. By the time we got home it was raining hard. We switched on the television to see if there were any tornado warnings for our area. There were none, so I decided this dark and stormy night was a good time to write. At the special request of one of my readers, I was writing a column about squirrels for our local paper. I picked up where I had left off before supper. The column did not jell earlier, and it wasn't working now. How long would I sit at the computer before the words fell into place?

It was only 7 P.M., but it looked more like 10 P.M. Thunder rumbled and zigzag lightning slashed the sky. Rain pelted my office windows. Up on the roof there arose such a clatter that I sprang from my chair to see what was the matter. Acting on impulse, I grabbed my owling light and binoculars as I rushed to the front door. Dime-size hail bounced off the roof. Suddenly, I looked over the driveway and saw a large bird silhouetted against the sky. Seeking refuge from the storm, it flew straight to a limb high in the elm tree in my front yard.

At first I thought it was an Eastern Screech-Owl. What night bird, other than an owl, is that size? When I turned my high-powered spotlight on it, I saw its huge eyes glowing with an eerie luminescence. I couldn't remember ever seeing an owl's eyes glow like that. The bird was resting on the limb in a horizontal position, so then I knew it was not an owl. Owls perch upright. So what kind of bird was it? Was it a Common Nighthawk? I had seen them on spring and summer evenings hawking insects in my neighborhood, but I had never seen their eyes glow.

Juggling the heavy spotlight and my binoculars, I saw that the bird was mottled and buff-brown all over. Could it be a Chuck-will's-widow? I had never seen one in my yard. Southern cousin of the Whip-poor-will, the chuck is a denizen of the night, more often heard than seen, with endless whistled repetitions of its name. In my twenty-four years of birding, I had heard hundreds of chucks calling in the night and seen them in the daytime only twice. In the darkness of the storm how could I make a positive identification? I headed back to my office for a book.

Again at the front door and trying to stay out of the rain, I leaned against the doorjamb, my binoculars in one hand and spotlight in the other. In the light's beam I saw sparkling raindrops bouncing off the bird's head and back. It fluffed its feathers and shook its head vigorously, sending droplets of water in all directions. Sharlande read aloud the description of Chuck-will's-widow in Harry C. Oberholser's *The Bird Life of Texas:* "its presence most frequently announced by its chuck-will's-widow call. Eyes of both sexes glow like live coals in flashlight beam." Ah ha! Good clue, but I needed more, since this bird was silent. Then Sharlande read the description of Common Nighthawk: "lacks rictal bristles and brilliant 'eyeshine' for which its close relatives are famous."

Okay. We knew our bird had "brilliant eyeshine," but what about "rictal bristles"? It was time for the spotting scope. The sky had gone from light to dark and back to light again. I opened the storm door as wide as I could, fixed the latch at the top so it would stay open, and set up the scope. When the foot-long bird came into focus it filled the frame. On its neck I saw "rictal bristles," stiff feathers that funnel flying insects into the bird's wide gape. Now we knew for sure it was a Chuck-will's-widow.

When the sky lightened, a Northern Mockingbird began singing in our front yard as if it were dawn. We could not believe our ears when it mimicked the call of a Chuck-will's-widow, as if confirming our identifi-cation. For a grand finale after the forty-five-minute show, our mysteri-ous bird spread its twenty-four-inch, blunt, rounded wings, lifted silently into fluttering flight, and disappeared into the night. I had my column. The squirrels would have to wait.

As Annie Dillard says, "When the Muse comes, she doesn't tell you to write; she says, get up for a minute, I've got something to show you, stand here."

Had I not gotten up from my computer at precisely the second I did and gone to the front door when I heard hail (the Muse) hitting my roof, I would have missed seeing this mystical bird and the column would have been about squirrels. Now, you probably think I made up what I said about the mocker. Well, you're really going to think I made this up: While reading my column the following Saturday, my husband called me into the living room in time to hear the mocker in the front yard once again mimicking the chuck.

The following Tuesday, the Muse came again in the form of a phone call. The squirrels would just have to wait. Wayne and Aggie Poe, some friends who read my column, called to say that they had found a Chuck-will's-widow on May 20. It was nesting at the site where they were build-ing a house a few miles from Crawford, Texas. They wondered if I would like to see it. Were they kidding?

The next morning I met Wayne and Aggie on the highway a few miles from their home, transferred all my gear to their car, and they took me to the site. I never would have found the place alone. When we arrived at the scene I got the spotting scope, binoculars, and camera out of the car and followed the Poes. Not wanting to disturb the bird, we stopped about forty feet from the nesting place.

Chucks don't actually construct nests. The female finds a depression among dead leaves on the forest floor and lays her eggs in it. The day the Poes discovered the nest they saw two glossy, elliptical eggs, so naturally we were looking for the eggs. The chuck is a master of camouflage. Its cryptic plumage blends perfectly with the leaf litter and its surround-ings. Aggie and Wayne both had difficulty relocating the bird on the nest. Wayne finally spotted it and gave me directions so I could get it in the scope.

Wow! What a picture! There sat the bird, filling the viewfinder, yet it was so well camouflaged that it was all we could do to distinguish its chunky form from the dry oak leaves. Even after seeing the chuck in the scope I could not believe this was happening. In twenty-four years of birding I had seen only two chucks. Now, in less than two weeks, my count was up to four.

We tried to sneak closer, but the bird flushed. With great effort it lifted its awful bulk off the nest. A twenty-four-inch wingspan looks enormous at close range. The chuck flew clumsily a short distance, as if on broken wings, before flopping back to the ground, intentionally distracting us the way a Killdeer does. The mystical bird didn't make a sound but drew itself to full height, swaying back and forth like an owl, its eyes fixed on our eyes. Every few minutes it laboriously flew another short distance, each time dropping heavily back to the ground.

Not wanting our human scent to attract predators to the area, we moved back to our original position. With binoculars and scope, we searched for the glossy eggs among the leaves. Sharp-eyed Wayne quietly announced that two downy chicks were huddled together on the leaf litter, surprising all of us. Their precocial down exactly matched the dead brown oak leaves. By our calculations, the chicks had hatched either that day or the day before. To quote John Muir, they were "so fine and beautiful," they "might well fire the dullest observer to desperate enthusiasm."

Soon after we moved away from the chicks, the mother was back at the nest brooding them. We left with the hope that predators would have an even more difficult time than we did finding these "fine and beautiful" wonders of nature. Hopefully they would not find them at all. ❧

Yertle the Kingbird

If I could sit high, how much greater I'd be!
What a king! I'd be ruler of all I could see!
—Dr. Seuss, Yertle the Turtle

The birds on the TV antenna behind the KWTX studio in Waco must have felt like Yertle the Turtle when they chose their nest site atop the 220-foot tower. Why, they could probably see "forty miles from their throne in the sky."

From his office at ground level, Kirby Pope, an engineer at Channel 10, operates cameras mounted atop this tall perch. Early one summer morning, Kirby did a double take when he panned the camera and a bowl-shaped structure of twigs and grass in which two downy chicks nestled popped into view. Kirby left the camera running for more than an hour while two adult birds made numerous trips with grasshoppers for the nestlings. Ray Deaver, the station's president and general manager, took the tape to his wife, Ellen, an avid birder and friend of mine. Since I was ill that week, I had not even turned on the television and so knew nothing about the birds until Ellen called. She asked if Ray could drop off the tape so I could confirm the birds' identity.

After viewing the tape, I called Ellen and Mike Barger, one of the newscasters, and told them the birds were Western Kingbirds (*Tyrannus verticalis*). No doubt about it! Throughout the next week, Central Texans saw live coverage of the birds during each weather segment. Weatherman Rusty Garrett said he spoke to schoolchildren in a neighboring town that week and all they wanted to know about were "the birds."

When Kirby took over the cameras at 5 A.M. the next Monday, one fully feathered baby teetered precariously on the side of the nest, stretching its wings. Kirby looked again at 7 A.M. and his heart almost stopped. The nest was empty. He went outside to search for the babies and found only one. The tiny bird's maiden voyage must have been a doozy. Yet somehow it managed to land safely on the soft grass 220 feet below its penthouse launch pad. With the parents hovering about, Kirby placed the fledgling in a safe spot and returned to his office. On the 5 o'clock news, the newscaster announced that the birds had flown from the nest. "Bye, bye, birdies."

I jumped in the car and headed for the TV station. When I arrived on the scene at 5:30 P.M., two adult Western Kingbirds were flying near the crepe myrtle bushes in front of the station. One of them darted low, caught an insect and stuffed it into the red gaping mouth of the baby on the ground, which I had not seen until then. When I wasn't looking, the parents coaxed the fledgling into one of the bushes. Slowly, I crept toward them, wanting to find the baby's hiding place. Fluttering above the bush and calling loudly, both parents acted as if they were ready to take on all five feet five inches of me if I came another step closer. I can take a hint. Kingbirds are notorious for attacking hawks and crows that venture too close, and I would not have been at all surprised if they had attempted to attack me, a mere human. They aren't called "tyrant" flycatchers for nothing. I retreated to the car and continued to watch from there with binoculars.

I was amazed to see that the young bird was a miniature replica of its parents. Though only two weeks old, it already had a pale gray head and breast, olive-gray upper parts, white throat, yellow belly, and white along each side of its square-tipped black tail—identical to both adults.

Is it unusual to see Western Kingbirds in Central Texas? No. They can be seen on utility wires, tree limbs, power poles, or fences in both the city and the country. You occasionally may see one drop to the ground, wrestle an insect, take it back to its perch, and eat it.

Is it rare for kingbirds to nest on such lofty pinnacles? Absolutely! I called the Ornithology Lab at Cornell University in Ithaca, New York, where nest records are kept. According to the definitive authority, *Life Histories of North American Birds*, Western Kingbirds normally nest in trees and shrubs from 16.4 feet to 76.8 feet above the ground. They may also nest on windmills, oil derricks, or transformer poles. Until now, however, there was no record of their nesting 220 feet above ground. Waco's Western Kingbirds may well hold the record for the highest nest.

Thanks to Waco's KWTX-TV, Central Texans were privileged to eavesdrop on this bit of "high" drama. With apologies to Dr. Seuss, in my imagination I hear the young kingbird in the crepe myrtle chanting: "I'm Yertle the Kingbird! Oh, marvelous me! For I am the ruler of all that I see!" 🐦

Rocks of Flobins

"What's the deal with all the robins?" "I see flocks of robins everywhere I go. Does this mean spring will be early this year?" I hear such questions and comments repeatedly every winter. I tell the inquirers that American Robins are doing exactly what they are supposed to do in winter: congregating in huge flocks. Bobbee Watts, who lives near me, commented that there were so many robins in her yard, she thought they might be holding a convention.

One of the best known birds in the United States, American Robin nests from the tree line in Alaska and northern Canada south to the Gulf Coast and the mountains of Mexico. Its scientific name is *Turdus migratorius. Turdus* is Latin for "thrush." The thrush family includes some of our most eloquent woodland songsters: Wood Thrush, Swainson's Thrush, Hermit Thrush, and Eastern Bluebird, to name but a few.

From its two-toned beak to its conspicuous dark brown, white-cornered tail, the ten-inch American Robin is the largest of the thrushes. *Migratorius,* Latin for "wandering," describes the robin's habit of traveling from one place to another in search of food. The old adage "Birds of a feather flock together" rings especially true with robins. The more eyes and ears in a group, the better the chances for individual birds to find new food sources.

This was demonstrated in living color in my backyard one January day. Sharlande, planting tulip bulbs in the front yard, needed a shovel. We tracked through the muddy backyard to find one. I noticed the wheelbarrow had collected rainwater the night before. Without thinking, I reached for the handles and started to dump the water, then on a whim decided to leave it and see "who" might find the two-inch pool.

As soon as Sharlande and I walked back inside, we looked out the window. A robin was already standing on the edge of the rusty wheelbarrow. It seemed to be trying to decide whether to take a dip. We grabbed our binoculars and spent the next four hours in front of the window, spellbound by the show. One, two, three, then four robins played musical chairs around the rim of the wheelbarrow. One stepped gingerly into the water, dipped its persimmon-colored breast into the pool, and splashed so vigorously I wondered if there would be any water left for the other birds. When fully saturated, the first robin hopped onto a low branch near the wheelbarrow and began to preen. Another and another followed suit, with never more than one bird bathing at a time.

Soon I noticed dozens more robins running and stopping across the lawn as robins do, turning their heads first to one side and then the other, as if looking or listening. With their bills they tossed leaves helter-skelter, like children on Christmas morning rummaging through piles of tissue paper, looking for one more gift. The "gifts" the robins found were plump yellow chinaberries that had fallen from the trees, worms in the moist earth, and insects in the brown grass. A robin with a chinaberry in its beak reminded me of Robin Williams's movie character Patch Adams with a rubber ball on his nose.

I looked toward my neighbor's garden and saw ten or twelve robins playing a game of "Who-can-jump-the-highest?" as they grabbed berries from the nandina bush. Their game did not last long. When the Northern Mockingbird who "owns" the bush discovered the marauders, he promptly sent the whole "rock of flobins" scampering back to worms and chinaberries.

During the show I saw a squirrel whose undertail matched the color of a robin's breast, White-winged Doves with a rosy gloss on the sides of their necks, scarlet male Northern Cardinals, Great-tailed Grackles with a bluish-purple sheen on their backs, a reddish-brown Carolina Wren in the woodpile, European Starlings decked out in their speckled iridescent winter plumage, a tiny Ruby-crowned Kinglet with red crown flashing, and a Yellow-rumped Warbler hawking insects and flashing its "butter rump."

Artists painting the scene would have had to dip their brushes into a color matching ripe persimmons or the inside of a baked sweet potato time and time again to catch the true hues of the squirrel's tail, the Carolina Wren's buff breast, the robin's breast, and the rusty wheelbarrow.

Before we knew it, the afternoon had flown. Suddenly, my backyard was devoid of the living color we had enjoyed. The birds dispersed to find a roosting place for the night—and so did we. ❧

Cardinals Flock, Too

To every thing there is a season,
and a time to every purpose under the heaven.
—Ecclesiastes 3:1

The Muse comes in different forms in different seasons. One week in November it came as a "Brrrrrrrrrring!"—the distinctive sound that breaks in on the net to inform you of an "Instant Message." It was Bob Griffin, then mayor of Hewitt, Texas. Bob's message read, "Noticed an unusually high number of cardinals lately. Any significance? I love to think they're here for my personal enjoyment. I've seen eighteen birds at a time with varying degrees of redness."

One winter evening I looked out my bird window and saw a spectacle not soon to be forgotten: ten pairs of Northern Cardinals foraging beneath the sunflower feeder in my backyard. It looked as if someone had scattered crimson blossoms on my lawn. Although I shall long remember the scene, it is not unusual during late fall and winter to see four to sixty or more cardinals in a group. They may be in your backyard, along a roadside, or in a wooded area.

It is the season for both cardinals and robins to flock—a rather common behavior after the end of the breeding season, when the last of the juveniles have become independent. These flocks may contain a mixture of juveniles and adults, as in the Griffins's yard. Juvenile cardinals are rather dingy and some of them still have dark bills in the fall. These mixed flocks remain together throughout the winter and break up in February or March. Often, large numbers of cardinals will perch in an evergreen, magically transforming an ordinary juniper into an extraordinary vision. As the Irish say, this is truly a "feast of seeing."

Flocking has its advantages. Because a flock has more eyes and ears than an individual, protection against predators is more reliable. A bird in a flock is less likely to be surprised by an accipiter (a bird-eating hawk) or an owl or other predators than when it is alone. Go to any woodland edge in fall or winter and imitate the call of an Eastern Screech-Owl. Usually, a mixed flock of curious birds, including several cardinals, will come out of hiding to "mob" the intruder. If an owl is actually present, it may be intimidated by such numbers and move to a different perch, but it seldom leaves its territory.

In addition to predator defense, flocking birds are less likely to overlook food sources than when alone, whether sunflower seeds at your backyard feeder or the natural foods that are abundant during fall and winter months. Additionally, members of a flock may discover new food sources, which can make the difference between life and death during the cold winter months. A cardinal can normally carry about three days' worth of reserve fat—enough to get it through an average ice storm or blizzard. If it can't find food by the fourth day, it begins to starve, and death follows swiftly. If it is in a flock, this is not likely to happen.

Most backyard birds come to our feeders to stock up shortly before retiring for the night. Two of the most energy-rich foods you can offer cardinals (and other seed-eating birds) are black-oil sunflower seeds and suet or suet mixes. This is the fuel that stokes their fire, so to speak. A bird can keep its flame alive only so long as the fuel lasts. Like humans, birds huddle together to draw warmth from each other's bodies. The more birds there are roosting (sleeping) together during severely cold weather, the warmer the individuals will be. At dusk you may see Northern Cardinals flying singly or in large groups to their roosts, which are often in dense evergreen thickets.

Enjoy the season of the flocking cardinals in your backyard or wherever you see them, for I believe that in a way they are here for our personal enjoyment. Accept the gift and be thankful. Bob Griffin died a few months after his Instant Message came "Brrrrrrring-ing" to me through cyberspace. I'm grateful the cardinals provided Bob with a feast of seeing during his last days on this earth. §➤

The Bird with the Sky on His Back

The bird on the wire was sitting like a bluebird: upright, but a little hunched at the shoulders. The morning sun backlighting the bird made it impossible to see its color. I was somewhat skeptical about a bluebird in that location, never having seen one in that area before. Then I heard that unmistakable soft, lilting warble, "chur-churlee-churlee," and knew it was an Eastern Bluebird.

A few years ago, while driving past the Heart of Texas Soccer Complex in Waco, a flash of blue startled me. When I turned around and went back, I noticed a hole near the top of the wooden gatepost at the entrance to the soccer fields. Thousands of people use that gate during the soccer season, so I concluded it was an impossible place for bluebirds to nest. Nevertheless, after watching the post for a short time I saw a female Eastern Bluebird enter the hole.

During the next few weeks I returned to the soccer complex when no soccer games were in progress. Using my car as a blind, I watched the activity around the nest hole. Both parents fed the nestlings, bringing countless grasshoppers and other bugs for their offspring, and then taking away white fecal sacs after the babies were fed. I don't remember how many young fledged that year, but for years afterward, until a metal pole replaced the wood post, Eastern Bluebirds nested in that unlikely spot.

Inquisitive bluebirds have little fear of people and investigate a variety of unusual nest sites: newspaper tubes, freight-car couplers, abandoned chipmunk dens, rural mailboxes, clothespin bags, inactive Cliff Swallow nests, rock crevices, tin cans, stovepipes, horse trailers, bumpers, car grills, the empty gas tanks of old tractors, boots left on top of cars at campsites, and the tailpipes of abandoned cars. It seems any old cavity will do.

Historically, bluebirds nested in natural cavities in dead trees or abandoned woodpecker holes. When the early settlers of our country put up wooden fences, the hollows in fence posts provided new nest sites for bluebirds. Later, when landowners began cutting dead trees for firewood and farmers replaced wooden fence posts with metal ones, bluebirds experienced fierce competition for nest sites from two ubiquitous species that are not natives of this country: House Sparrows and European Starlings. After that, bluebird numbers drastically declined. Had humans not intervened and started hundreds of Bluebird Trails across the country, we probably would not enjoy the presence of these lovely birds today.

Of the three species of bluebirds in North America (Eastern, Western, and Mountain), the easterns are the only ones that nest where I live in

Central Texas. The male Eastern Bluebird sports cobalt blue on his head, wings, back, and tail. His throat, breast, and flanks are cinnamon orange, and his belly and undertail are white. The female is a duller version of the male.

Offer the right type of birdhouse in the proper habitat, and it is fairly easy to attract bluebirds to nest boxes. (For the size and location of boxes, contact the North American Bluebird Society in Darlington, Wisconsin.) Open areas of two to five acres with scattered trees, little or no understory, and sparse ground cover are important. As you drive through the country, watch for bluebirds fluttering from perches on wires or fences, catching grasshoppers or katydids in short grass and returning to their perches.

Once you attract bluebirds to nest boxes, it is easier to entice them to feeders and birdbaths. Their favorite foods are berries, insects, and mealworms (available at bait stores and bird supply stores). Bluebirds also accept peanut hearts, pecan meats, suet peanut butter mixes, and bakery products. Place these on bird tables or tray feeders near the nest boxes at first. After the birds get used to them, gradually move the feeders closer to the house for better viewing. Bluebirds drink and bathe in ponds, streams, and birdbaths.

Henry David Thoreau, a nineteenth-century naturalist, aptly described this azure beauty as the bird that "carries the sky on his back." If you live in the proper habitat for bluebirds, do whatever it takes to attract these charming birds. The rewards of seeing splashes of blue in your backyard will far outweigh your greatest efforts. ❧

The Chickadee

BY HAROLD OSBORNE

I think that I shall never see
A bird quite like the chickadee.
His constant chatter, his wee black cap
Bridge o'er the unbridged language gap.

He quickly flits, he seldom sits.
He scatters widely birdseed pits.
He eats upright or upside down.
His antics make him quite a clown.

And though we seldom do converse,
The chickadee helps to disperse
The loneliness I often find
Afflicting much of humankind.

I have to laugh when I watch him play
On treetop branch or feeding tray.
I often think the chickadee
Was God's own special gift to me. ❧

Chick-a-dee-dee-dee-dee

"Chick-a-dee-dee-dee-dee." The familiar call of the Carolina Chickadee draws my attention to a small, acrobatic bird that flits from red oak to sunflower feeder, steals a seed, and flies quickly to the elm tree in my front yard. Holding the prize between its feet against the limb, it hammers away with its short, stout, pointed bill until the heart of the seed is uncovered. After swallowing the kernel it flies back to the feeder for another seed, then another and another. You may see chickadees feeding upside down as often as you see them right side up.

Scenarios similar to this are repeated many times a day throughout the year at feeders almost everywhere across the United States and Canada into Alaska. Chickadees of one sort or another just about cover the continent, for there are seven species nationwide. All of them sing some rendition of their name. The two most widely distributed and best known are the Carolina and Black-capped Chickadees.

Chickadees are some of America's favorite birds. Their small size, black cap and bib, baby face, constant chatter, friendliness, and curiosity endear them to us. When you read about hand-feeding and -taming wild birds, chickadees are among the first birds mentioned. One book claims anyone who can sit or stand still for five or ten minutes can hand-tame a wild bird at the feeder.

Once, at a picnic area near Rocky Mountain National Park, our son Sam, then seven years old, was enchanted by Black-capped Chickadees feeding from his hand. Having a supply of sunflower seeds in the car, we were prepared for the chickadees, which are so accustomed to humans. These friendly, intensely active little birds were unafraid when Sam, standing still as a Douglas fir, offered seeds from his outstretched hand. Sam, thirty-two at the time of this writing, still remembers the way the chickadee's tiny, cold feet felt on his palm.

It is easy to attract chickadees to your yard. Although they will eat almost anything, their preferences include black-oil sunflower seed, sunflower hearts, suet, suet mixes, peanut butter mixed with cornmeal or flour, small nutmeats, peanuts, and doughnuts. They accept food in a variety of feeders: tubular feeders with perches, window trays, plastic spheres with seed holes, and hopper feeders. Sometimes they even drink from hummingbird feeders.

Fortunately, I was looking out the window one day when a Carolina Chickadee that was investigating some new feeders in my yard accidentally got its leg caught where two offset hanging hooks join. I rushed outside to rescue the struggling bird. Looking me straight in the eye with bright, sparkling eyes, it didn't seem afraid as I gently lifted its fragile leg to freedom. It is hard to imagine just how small a chickadee is until you have that half-ounce ball of feathers in your hand. My friend Rufus Spain came over and fashioned a small wooden wedge so no other bird is likely to have the same mishap.

Chickadees prefer to nest in natural cavities. A friend who was having her trees trimmed brought a chickadee nest to show me. The trimmers inadvertently cut across the top of the nest, a deep, perfectly round bowl excavated in the rotten center of the limb. The only nest material was human hair. My friend remembered that she had cut her daughter's hair in the backyard a few weeks prior to the tree trimming. The female chickadee apparently found the child's hair to be just what she needed for the soft, welcoming center of her nest. Unfortunately, the tree-trimmers didn't know until they sliced through the limb that the nest with five newly hatched chicks was hidden inside. What is the lesson in this? Don't prune your trees until nesting season is over. You'll love having these acrobatic feathered midgets as neighbors, for chickadees are wonderfully entertaining. Indeed, I often think the chickadee was "God's own special gift to me." ❧

Guess Who's Coming to Dinner

From time to time I find a pile of feathers here and a pile of feathers there, across my yard. When that happens, it isn't too hard to guess who's been coming to dinner. An uninvited guest comes to our yard to dine about the same time every year. Though its exact arrival date can't be foreseen, our guest's behavior is predictable. Seemingly from nowhere, a Sharp-shinned Hawk appears. The jays, cardinals, and chickadees, feeding quietly moments before, squawk and spring for cover. Suddenly, as if a master switch is flipped, all is still; all is silent in the backyard.

"Sharpy" swoops down and lands on the same branch as he did the year before and the year before that. Shifting from one foot to the other, he waits for a small bird to reveal its whereabouts. It doesn't matter to the sentry how long it takes. He has nothing better to do.

Looking from side to side with piercing eyes, he searches the hedge below. Detecting the slightest quiver of a leaf, the hunter drops to the attack feet first, much as an Osprey splashes into a lake for a fish. He emerges from the hedge a moment later, the prize clutched in his talons. He carries the squealing bird to the ground. He kneads the small body with needle-sharp claws, like a baker preparing dough for the oven. Life slowly oozes from the bird, and once again there is silence. Leaving only feathers and skull, the hawk devours his feast on the spot or carries it to a nearby tree. In less than half an hour the drama is over—over until hunger again attacks the attacker.

My first encounter with a bird-eating hawk was many years ago. At the time I had no understanding of nature's law. I saw only death, not the process of life and death. At first I hated the bird of prey and tried to rescue its victims. However, during the long process of observing the hunter, I gained unexpected insight.

From time to time I saw Sharpy consume goldfinches, juncos, and mockingbirds. Why couldn't the accipiter take only House Sparrows? I wondered. There was an overabundance of them. At first this troubled me (and still does, to a degree); but then I realized I was no longer trying to rescue the birds. I at last understood the predator's niche in the overall scheme: a hawk's consumption of beautiful songbirds is as much a part of nature's balance as its eating of the pesky ones. Someone has defined a predator as being "any creature that beats you to another creature you wanted." I decided that the least I could do was provide cover for small birds so they would have a sporting chance.

One day I watched in awe as a hawk drank and bathed from my back-door neighbor's three-tiered birdbath. I had never seen a bird of prey at a birdbath before. When I first spotted it from my kitchen window, the hawk was standing on the ground, seemingly in no hurry to leave. Hoping to get a better look, I went for my spotting scope. When I returned to the window, the hawk was on the rim of the lowest tier of the birdbath. I determined from its size and plumage that it was an immature female Cooper's Hawk, another bird-eating hawk.

Looking around to make sure no one was about, she bent double and drank deeply from the basin. She must have been very thirsty because she repeated this several times in the next ten minutes. Then, discovering the water cascading from the top tier, she opened her beak and let the liquid pour in. She let the droplets run down her front, fluffed out her breast feathers, tilted her head backward, and then stood there as if sighing with pleasure. For that brief moment she knew she was at the top of the food chain in that backyard and need not worry about her own safety. If she were capable of a thought process, she must have thought she had found her own private spa.

Whether it's a hummingbird at her nest, a jackrabbit scurrying across a field, or an unexpected guest coming for dinner in my backyard, I find a special fascination in watching wild creatures going about the business of everyday living. ᐟᕙ

Of Juncos and Keiflins

Three days before Christmas I was making my family's favorite holiday cookies, *keiflins* (pronounced "KIFF-lins"), from a German recipe that has been in my family for five generations. I don't remember a single Christmas of my life without *keiflins,* although I've had two near misses. I was in San Angelo several weeks before Christmas, 1995, taking care of our son Van, who was seriously ill. Arriving back home in Waco at 6 P.M. on Christmas Eve, I was greeted at the front door by the grandkids asking, "When are you going to make the *keiflins?* " That night, our granddaughter Kelsey and I sat up until 1 A.M. rolling the crescent-shaped cookies in our hands, baking them, and smothering them in powdered sugar. Although I was totally exhausted that night, I was happy for the opportunity to pass on this family tradition to Kelsey.

The second near miss was when Van's wife Peggy was dying of cancer in December, 1998. Again, I was in San Angelo with Van. At the time I didn't have the heart to make *keiflins;* but Sam, who was living in Seattle, came through. He couldn't stand to think of his mother without *keiflins* on Christmas Day, no matter what the circumstances. He mailed a batch of those buttery, sweet cookies that tasted of home and comfort to me. They arrived in the nick of time on Christmas Eve.

Another year, while shaping the dough in my hands, I looked out the window and saw yet another sure sign of Christmas: four small, gray birds beneath the feeder. Hoping to get a better look, I picked up the binoculars

Junco eating a pile of keiflins, by Mike.

that are always lying on the table next to the window. Just as I had hoped, the birds were Dark-eyed Juncos, our special winter visitors.

For a long time, juncos, like "winter Texans" of the human variety, have been called "snowbirds" for two good reasons. One, their presence usually portends snow, or at least colder weather. Two, their plumage matches the mood of a snowy day: dark gray on top like the clouds, and snow-white underneath. Juncos sometimes forecast the weather with more accuracy than meteorologists. The only times I have recorded their presence in my yard have been right before a "blue norther." At our house, no Christmas is complete without *keiflins,* and no wintry blast without juncos.

Juncos have a knack for surviving severe weather. So long as natural foods are abundant in the wild, juncos stick to their countryside haunts. At the first hint of bad weather, however, they come back to our feeders. A bird bander and the author of *A Complete Guide to Bird Feeding,* John V. Dennis says juncos have an uncanny memory of exactly where food can be found during an emergency. The juncos Dennis has banded on his property in previous years usually lead the way for flocks returning to his feeding stations when the weather turns bad.

When I started birding in the 1970s, four forms of Dark-eyed Junco were recognized as separate species: Slate-colored, White-winged, Oregon, and Gray-headed. In 1973, scientists discovered juncos were breeding with one another at the edge of their ranges and lumped all four into one species, calling the group "Dark-eyed Junco."

Today there are fifteen described races of Dark-eyed Junco and six recognized subspecies, all similar in size, ranging from five to 6.6 inches in length. The six subspecies vary slightly in plumage characteristics. All exhibit a basic plumage form, predominantly gray above and white or pinkish below. When driving down a country road, you may see flocks of juncos flying up from the roadside, flashing white outer tail feathers, which all the subspecies flaunt. With a pink conical bill, pinkish brown legs, and darker feet, the Slate-colored Junco is the subspecies I see in Central Texas. In the males, the darker head, chest, and upper flanks form a hood. The female is brownish gray overall with buff flanks.

Preferring to feed on the ground, juncos' favorite food is white millet. Even though they are perching birds, some learn to hover at perchless log feeders containing suet or suet mixes. They also accept sunflower, peanut hearts, and bakery products. They probably would love *keiflins* if we ever had any left over. Keiflins and Juncos just seem to go together at Christmas.

Several days before Christmas one year, the TV weathermen vacillated back and forth about whether we would get an Arctic blast that week. They said one computer model showed we would get it and another that it would go north of us. Don't the weathermen know? All they have to do is call me. I'll tell them what the juncos are saying. Right now I'm going outside to cover all exposed pipes and bring in the outdoor plants. Never mind what the computer models say. My money is on the snowbirds. I may even sacrifice a few *keiflins* for them. ᕙ

Keiflin Recipe

I would love to share the *keiflin* recipe with you, but first I have to tell you the story of how my family obtained it. It was sometime in the early 1920s. We were living in Marvell, Arkansas, a small town near the Mississippi delta, where I was born in 1931. My mother's sister, whom we called Ebby, went to a Christmas party and was totally taken with the cookies a German lady had made. My aunt asked for the recipe and the woman finally agreed to sell it to her for twenty-five dollars on the condition that she would never give it to anyone else. That was a lot of money at the time. Of course, through the years Ebby couldn't keep such a good thing to herself, so she shared it with the whole family. The rest is history.

I work from my mother's handwritten copy of the recipe, which is almost all to pieces. Who knows how big her bottle of vanilla was or how much was a "pinch" of salt? I just pour in a good bit of vanilla, work it into the dough, and then taste the raw dough. If it tastes right, I know I've poured in enough. Here's the recipe:

2 sticks butter (softened to room temperature)
6 tablespoons powdered sugar (Heaping! And I do mean *heaping!*)
2½ cups flour
2 cups ground nuts (I use pecans.)

Pinch of salt
½ bottle Vanilla (enough to moisten batter)

Dump all ingredients in mixing bowl and go to work with your hands. Pinch balls the size of a marble, roll in hands, form crescents and place on ungreased cookie sheets. Bake twenty-five minutes at 325 degrees. (Check them after about twenty minutes. If they are already brown on the bottom, it's time to take them out.) After cookies have cooled on a rack, roll them in powdered sugar. Makes approximately ten dozen.

The Indomitable Killdeer

Infancy, we say, is hedged about by many perils;
but the infancy of birds is cradled and pillowed in peril.
—John Burroughs

The Killdeer (*Charadrius vociferus*) is a common bird with an uncommon knack for survival. That fact was brought home to me one day on a ranch near Waco, where I spotted a Killdeer sitting motionless in a pasture. Camera equipment resting on my shoulder, I crept to within a few yards of the Killdeer. Hearing a roar like thunder, I turned to see a cloud of dust. Dozens of horses were galloping across the pasture. Following them, cowhands whooped it up, waving hats over their heads. I half expected to hear a hearty, "Hi, ho, Silver! Away!"

In fear of being trampled, I raced for the car. When the dust settled I was surprised to see the Killdeer still sitting tightly on her shallow scrape of a nest. As soon as I had calmed down enough to pick up my camera and tripod again, I focused the telephoto lens on the brooding bird's head. I had never noticed the ring of orange skin outlining the bird's eye nor the way each feather is delicately edged in a soft contrasting color.

Through the lens I could see small bits of dirt on the bird's bill. Evidently, just before the roar of horses' hooves drowned out everything else, she had turned the eggs that nestled on bare earth beneath her and hadn't taken time to clean her bill. She stared at me in defiance as I stared at her in awe. Rising, with her tail partially spread like a feather headdress, she stood between me and three well-camouflaged eggs, crying, "Killdee-ah! Killdee-ah!"

It was then that I noticed another Killdeer nearby. Her mate called vociferously, demonstrating the reason behind their Latin name. He pretended to be injured, dragging one wing on the ground and flopping around as if in great pain—a ruse commonly employed by Killdeer (as well as some other birds) to lure intruders away from their nesting territories. His flopping and calling led me farther and farther away from the nest. Soon I retreated to the car and the birds returned to business as usual.

During the following weeks I observed the birds' nesting activities from the car and learned that both parents take an active part in the nesting process, including a twenty-four- to twenty-six-day incubation period and care and brooding of offspring. Soon after chicks break out of their eggs, the parents brood them until the chicks' downy feathers dry. Since they are precocial (fully feathered when born), young Killdeer are able to walk and feed themselves immediately after hatching. Unable to predict the hatching date, I missed seeing the downy babies scramble from the nest.

From the beginning, Killdeer chicks look like miniature adults with plumage almost identical to that of their parents. The main difference is one dark neck band on the young where the adults have two. The conscientious parents brood the chicks often during their first few days out of the nest, also at night and when it is raining. This kind of brooding becomes gradually less frequent until the young reach the age of five weeks when they are capable of caring for themselves. Until then, the chicks follow the parents around as if on tiny invisible wheels, trying their hardest to keep up. Searching for food, they mimic the adults in their habit of alternately running several paces, stopping suddenly as if looking and listening, then dabbing at the ground with their bills.

Indomitable Killdeers often nest in odd places: driveways, airport runways, graveled rooftops, roadsides, and golf courses. Some have even been known to nest between the ties of a railroad track. I dare say, a pair of Killdeer choosing such a place probably encounters no more danger from passing trains than a pair of Killdeer on a Central Texas ranch encounters from galloping horses at roundup time. Perhaps the highly adaptable Killdeer's success as a species is due in part to its dogged determination to raise its young under the most adverse conditions. One thing is certain: the Killdeer is a survivor. ᔐ

Beep! Beep!

A large brown and white streaked bird lowered its tail, extended its neck to its full length and scooted across the road straight as an arrow in front of the Elderhostel van I was driving. I imagined its moving on wheels instead of feet, clouds of dust following the bird as it honked, "Beep! Beep!" with Wile E. Coyote in hot pursuit. However, rather than the comedic character of cartoon fame, this was the genuine real-life article, a Greater Roadrunner. Upon seeing it, most of my passengers called in unison, "John! There's your roadrunner!" Where was John? In the back of the van, fast asleep. From Massachusetts, John had never been to the Texas Hill Country, and at the beginning of the week he declared, "If I don't see another bird, I'll be happy if I see one roadrunner." Needless to say, John missed his most-wanted bird. By the time he woke up, the roadrunner had disappeared.

Almost everyone I know has a roadrunner story. Shannon Davies, my editor, told me she often sees roadrunners in her backyard in urban Austin. For a week, Shannon and her husband George had been enchanted by an orb spider spinning her "Charlotte's web" outside their bedroom window. They were relaxing at home one Sunday when suddenly a loud thump rattled the window blinds. When Shannon looked up, she saw a roadrunner standing inches from the window looking like the proverbial cat that had swallowed the canary. He had jumped several feet in the air and eaten the orb spider they had been watching with so much interest.

One April, while I was resident birder at Neal's Lodges in Concan, I looked out the café window one evening and saw a roadrunner scrambling into the bushes to catch a lizard. Soon it was back on the café patio, hopping from one picnic tabletop to the next, a lizard dangling from its long beak. Stopping in the middle of a table, it gulped the small lizard headfirst down the hatch. It couldn't have been better timing. A large birding group from up East had just arrived for supper. Most of them had never seen a roadrunner. The crowd inside the café gave the bird a standing ovation and asked what magic button I had punched to make the bird appear and give such a superb textbook performance.

The next day, while reading outside my cabin next door to the café, I suddenly became aware of movement in the live oak above me. Looking up from my book, I saw a long tail bobbing up and down. Lifting binoculars to my eyes, I discovered a Greater Roadrunner moving slowly from branch to branch. With wings flicking like a kinglet's, it cocked its head and looked first this way and then that, as if examining each limb from every possible angle. The stealthy way it moved over the limbs reminded me of its close cousin, the Squirrel Cuckoo of Latin America. After a few minutes it glided to the ground, ran across the grass, and disappeared over the rock wall overlooking the Frio River.

Ann Cunningham told me she had seen a roadrunner at the far edge of her property near Crawford, Texas, and wondered how she could entice it nearer to her house. Knowing Ann had an aversion to catching lizards and grasshoppers to offer the bird, I suggested she try to lure it with hotdogs or hamburger meat. Ann strewed small hotdog chunks, like Hansel and Gretel's trail of crumbs, from the fence to the back of the house. It worked!

After the roadrunner started making regular forays for hotdogs, Ann named him "Bubba." During the spring, Ann watched Bubba catch yellow butterflies on the wildflowers in her yard. In mid-June, Bubba brought his mate and offspring for a visit. Often she saw the little family sand bathing in a rocky/sandy place between the junipers and running and chasing each other about the yard like children playing tag. One day, Bubba ventured to one of the birdbaths in Ann's yard, stood on the rim, lowered his head, and dipped his stout beak into the water for a long drink. He then tilted his head back and allowed the water to slide down his throat.

A few weeks later, when the Cunninghams painted their porch, they moved Ann's collection of birdhouses from the porch to the yard. Once, when they looked up, Bubba was strutting around among the birdhouses, scrutinizing each one as though trying to decide which house to buy at this bizarre "yard sale."

I know it is anthropomorphic to attribute human characteristics to birds. But let's face it: the Greater Roadrunner has personality. To me, it is one of the most entertaining birds in the avian kingdom. §

The Cedar Bird

The tight-knit flock of birds, wheezing high-pitched, sibilant notes, circled above the winter-bare elm tree as one body, landing en masse. The well-groomed birds perched close together, erect and motionless, like toy soldiers ready to parade.

It was just the sort of cold, damp day on which I usually see my first Cedar Waxwings of the season. Droplets of water hung from every branch of the tree, icicles about to form. Clumps of bright green mistletoe loaded with plump white berries, delicious to birds but poisonous to humans, decorated the tree like giant Christmas balls. The birds fed on the berries without aggression. A bond of fellowship seemingly prevailed, dictating that each bird had equal rights to its share of the feast. But almost before I could say "*Bombycilla cedrorum*," all the berries had been stripped from the clumps of mistletoe.

When a flock of waxwings finds a tree or shrub loaded with fruit, the tree becomes a veritable banquet hall. The waxwings swarm like bees around the hanging berries, sometimes hovering to grab a bite. Individual birds often gorge themselves until they are so full they can't fly away. If the fruit is overripe and fermented, waxwings may become intoxicated and tumble from the tree and have to sober up on the ground before they can fly. Some even die from this intoxication.

After their feast in my front yard, I was surprised to see the birds lower their heads and turn upside down to drink the water droplets suspended under the limbs. Then, as if on command, the Cedar Waxwings dropped to the street beneath the tree where dozens of American Robins were drinking and bathing in puddles of rainwater.

In order to entice waxwings to your yard, you might want to offer a water feature. Water may be more attractive to Cedar Waxwings than food offerings. Like all fruit eaters, waxwings seem to have an unquenchable thirst.

Once they find your birdbath, it is entertaining to watch the bath-time ritual of a flock of these elegant birds. They flutter down from the tree-tops like miniature helicopters and encircle the water dish. They resemble mechanical toys, bowing and dipping for a drink, one after the other. After satisfying their thirst, they take turns going into the water for a thorough bathing. The scene could easily be set to music.

One of the most interesting and amusing behaviors among waxwings is when they perch on a utility wire or tree limb and pass a berry or other small fruit from one bird to the next, beak to beak, as if playing a game. Finally, one bird claims the prize and eats it. It is thought that this may be part of their courtship ritual.

Cedar Waxwings are dapper little birds that winter all across the southern United States. They are year-round residents in the northern half of the country and nest all over Canada. With silky, sleek plumage in soft shades of brown, gray, and yellow, they are among the most beautiful of North American birds and always look well groomed. With long, tufted crests, square yellow-tipped tails, white undertail coverts, dark bibs, rakish black "Zorro" masks outlined in white, and red tips on grayish wings, they are easy to identify. The wingtips look as if they have been dipped in red wax, which is where the species gets its common name. The sexes are alike, except the female's bib may be brown and the male's black. Waxwings have no seasonal variation in plumage.

Cedar Waxwings are gregarious. You hardly ever see just one. Notorious for wandering, they travel in large flocks throughout the year and appear to be nonterritorial. Their movements are totally unpredictable, typical of birds that feed on patchily distributed foods such as fruits. Consider yourself fortunate, indeed, if waxwings decide to grace your yard with their elegant presence. But be forewarned: Don't park your car under the tree where they are feeding or you will have to make a quick trip to the nearest carwash. ❧

King of the Hill

The Northern Mockingbird in our neighborhood acts as if he is "King of the Hill." Standing on our neighbor's TV antenna or the roof of our house, he surveys his kingdom. From these lofty perches, he fearlessly defends his winter feeding territory: holly and nandina bushes loaded with bright red berries. When this long, streamlined gray bird rushes to the attack, its white wing patches and outer tail feathers flash like signal flags. Woe unto anyone, man or beast, who comes near its food source. Intruders may include cats, dogs, birds of all kinds, mail carriers, neighbors, and above all, other mockingbirds.

Formerly considered a southern bird, *Mimus pollyglottos* is now known as the Northern Mockingbird to distinguish it from its tropical cousins living in Latin America. No longer exclusively southern, the Northern Mockingbird has greatly expanded its range northward in recent decades due in part to bountiful backyard feeders. The mocker now ranges widely over the North American continent, from southern Canada to Mexico and the West Indies and from southeastern Maine west to northern California. Although it is a permanent resident in its breeding territory, mockers living in the northern states withdraw southward during the winter only far enough to wait out the frigid weather.

It is not unusual for a single mockingbird to engage an entire flock of robins if they are making inroads on its berry or fruit supply. Such battles are not without purpose. In a relatively short time other birds can devour enough food to sustain one or two mockingbirds all winter. So when you see a mocker acting bold, daring, or tenacious during the winter, remember that it is only defending its link to survival.

I found out by accident that mockers love fruitcake. Since I am the only one at our house who likes fruitcake, at least half of the one I buy for Christmas is left after the holidays. One day I put a chunk of one in the wire basket that hangs in front of my writing window and voila! The mocker thought it was the most wonderful Christmas gift he had ever received. One year, when we tasted the figgy pudding a friend brought for Christmas dinner, we discovered she had left out the baking soda. Much to our dismay, the dessert was not fit for human consumption. The next day the mockingbird was delighted to find another Christmas treat in his basket. Two days later the mocker sat on an empty feeder, turned his head toward the window and did one of those scolding jobs mockers do so well. I knew his expletives were directed at me. Feeling sufficiently rebuked, I went outside and refilled the basket.

The avian emblem of five states—Texas, Florida, Arkansas, Tennessee, and Mississippi—"*Mimus polyglottos*" (many-tongued mimic) lives up to its scientific name. In addition to its own songs and calls, records show it can imitate almost forty species of birds and an untold number of nonbird sounds such as squeaky gates, wolf whistles, dog barks, hen cackles, car horns, and even a piano.

Once I heard the mocker in our neighborhood going through his repertoire of imitations. Right in the middle he suddenly came out with a startling, "Beep! Beep!" I remember thinking he must have overheard someone's television on a Saturday morning when Wile Coyote was chasing the roadrunner in one of their relentless battles. Then I remembered that Robert Goode, a teenager living across the street from us, had a new Volkswagen that he delighted in driving up and down our street and honking his horn—"Beep! Beep!"—at everyone he saw. Robert is presently a medical doctor in Seattle.

So expert are the mocker's imitations that electronic analysis cannot detect the difference from the original sounds. For years I have kept a list of birds I've heard our mocker imitate. My list of over twenty birds proves the Northern Mockingbird is not only a fantastic mimic but a splendid songster as well.

Late one spring afternoon many years ago I was out walking our dog Boo when I came upon a mockingbird singing a quiet evening song from his perch on a telephone pole. He was going through a rather lengthy repertoire, so I stopped to enjoy the concert. During one of the mocker's few pauses I heard a Carolina Wren singing in the distance. The mocker picked up on the wren's song and repeated it exactly. That gave me an idea: Since I do a pretty fair imitation of a Tufted Titmouse, I whistled its "Peter! Peter! Peter!" call. Without hesitation, the mocker answered with a perfect titmouse rendition. We repeated our exchange again and again. Each time the mocker responded with the same number of "Peters" I whistled. We enjoyed the game for several moments and then he returned to his evening song. The dog and I resumed our walk down the street.

A few minutes later, when Boo and I returned to the place where the mocker perched, he was still singing. I decided to try something different to see what the mimic would do. During one of his brief intermissions I whistled an unbirdlike, high-pitched, descending slur. To my surprise, *Mimus* repeated it precisely. I tried again, and again he echoed the sound. I didn't want to push my luck, so I decided to leave him to his own private concert. As I turned to leave, I said, "A pleasant evening to you, Sir. I enjoyed your performance." I half expected him to reply, "And a pleasant evening to you." ❧

Companions on the Way

When fall migration is in full swing, not only are birds of many species on the move to their winter homes, but Monarch butterflies are also flitting above our heads by the thousands on their way from Canada to a few high, cool, forested slopes west of Mexico City. Migration is quite possibly the most awe-inspiring phenomenon on the planet. How on Earth does a creature the size of my thumb fly nonstop across the Gulf of Mexico twice each year between winter and summer homes? The Ruby-throated Hummingbird, one of our flying jewels of summer, is that creature. I do not understand the mystery of its epic flight. Of all birds, however, the Arctic Tern is the world's migratory champion, circumnavigating the globe every year for a total of up to twenty-five thousand miles, roughly the same distance as the circumference of the world.

One fall day after a cool front came through Central Texas, Jan and Lynn Williams called to report hundreds of hawks on the ground in a plowed field next to the McGregor airport near Waco. They didn't need to describe the birds. I knew they were Swainson's Hawks. That's the way Swainson's Hawks rest during migration. They swirl around the heavens in "kettles" of hundreds or thousands, soaring from thermal to thermal, catching insects on the wing. Keen-eyed wind masters that they are, when they tire, they settle down for a night of rest, preferably in a plowed field where they will find insects and small mammals in abundance. They feed there until they are ready to move on, the next day if the hunting is good.

Since Swainson's Hawks excel in the art of soaring, they migrate overland by day to take advantage of the updrafts that give lift to their wings. They soar over open plains and prairies with up-tilted wings in teetering fashion, much the same as Turkey Vultures in flight. Virtually the entire population of Swainson's Hawks is migratory; on rare occasions a few have been known to winter in southern Florida and California's Central Valley. They breed in the grasslands of the western states and Canada and funnel through South Texas on their long odyssey from nesting grounds to winter homes as far south as the pampas of Argentina. Swainson's Hawks are the migratory champs in the hawk family. Traveling farther than any other hawk, their annual trip may take them from eleven thousand to seventeen thousand miles.

Neal Smith of the Smithsonian Tropical Research Institute in Panama has shown that Broad-winged and Swainson's Hawks, by carefully using thermal updrafts and other favorable air conditions, can soar overland from southern Texas and other southwestern regions of the United States, all the way to Central and South America in their annual migration. With this energy-saving type of flight, they travel thousands of miles on set wings without ever needing to stop and feed.

By the time I got to the plowed field near the McGregor airport that day, only a few Swainson's remained. I have seen the marvel of hundreds of hawks in a field on numerous occasions, so I didn't have to imagine what it had been like earlier that day. The huge flock was probably a mixture of dark- and light-phased Swainson's Hawks. Perhaps some Broad-winged Hawks had been mixed in with them. The two often travel together. More than likely, the hawks spent the morning following a tractor and eating crickets, grasshoppers, and small mammals turned up by the farmer's plow.

I pulled off the road to set up my spotting scope for a better look and soon spotted a light-phased Swainson's Hawk as it took flight from its hiding place on the other side of the fence. Spreading its long, narrow, pointed wings, it lifted effortlessly into the blue October sky. I saw the distinctive dark trailing edges on its underwings and the wide chestnut-brown band across its chest. Monarch butterflies, tiny orange creatures gently floating on the breeze, punctuated the azure sky through which the hawk sailed. That day I was witness to the tail end of two of the natural world's great spectacles performed by hawks and butterflies. Next time Jan and Lynn call, I'll try to be there earlier so I can catch the whole show. ❧

The Muse in Jogging Shoes

As mentioned in other chapters, the Muse sometimes comes in odd disguises: as hail bouncing off the roof, a tower-mounted TV camera panning the nest of a pair of flycatchers, a patch of rain-lilies on a rocky hillside, or the soft hoot of an owl. One August evening the Muse came in jogging shoes. Out for their evening exercise, two joggers glanced at the sky in time to see a huge flock of birds flying over. Not recognizing the winged creatures, the couple stopped at Kay Bond's house, up the street from where I live, on the outside chance that she might know the birds' identity. Not knowing what they were, Kay called me and suggested I go outside to see the mystery fliers and watch for two puzzled joggers heading my way.

I grabbed my binoculars and went outside. A huge "kettle" of birds of prey was swirling overhead on motionless wings. I didn't count them, but there must have been 150–200 falcon-shaped hawks, flying in circles like boiling water in a kettle, slowly, methodically, making their way north to south.

John and Melinda Quinius, jogging north to south down our street, arrived a few minutes later. Seeing me with binoculars, they stopped to ask if I knew what the birds were and why they were flying in such a large group. I told them they were Mississippi Kites, members of the hawk family, migrating from their breeding grounds as far north as southern Kansas all the way to South America for the winter. Some of the earliest fall migrants, kites often depart on their southerly odyssey by mid-August. Some occasionally winter as far north as southern Texas.

I went back inside the house to fetch a field guide so I could show John and Melinda a picture of the birds, then I handed them my binoculars. While they looked, I began to tell them about these graceful wind masters.

Mississippi Kites are uncommonly lovely. The first thing you notice is their great aerial agility. It is sheer poetry in motion. Sometimes appearing to be suspended in the sky, kites are well named for their buoyant flight, which is similar to that of a child's tissue-paper kite lazily floating through the air at the end of a string on the whim of the wind. Gliding on pointed, horizontal wings measuring nearly three feet from tip to tip,

Mississippi Kite in jogging shoes, by Mike.

Mississippi Kites sometimes suddenly break ranks to swoop down on a flying insect.

You may see them in urban areas as well as across the countryside. Kites seem most attracted to "tree islands" such as farm lots and shelterbelts, wherever insects are plentiful. Being insect specialists, their diet consists mostly of flying grasshoppers, dragonflies, beetles, cicadas, and crickets. Kites occasionally catch other aerial plankton in midair, including various bats and small birds. On the ground they may take small snakes, lizards, and frogs.

When seen in flight, the adult appears to be uniformly dark gray, both above and below, with a long, dark tail it frequently flares, and a light-colored head. Up close, the Mississippi Kite has a distinctive countenance with scarlet eyes staring out of a pronounced black mask. This highly migratory bird lives in North America approximately five months of the year, May to September, and ranges throughout the southern United States from the Carolina coasts to the Southwest plains. In recent years, the species has expanded its nesting range to New Mexico and selected areas of Arizona.

Fall flocks of Mississippi Kites like this one may be sizable and include three age groups: adults, yearlings, and the current year's juveniles. These kites follow an overland route, through Mexico and Central America, before finally arriving in central South America, their winter home. Keep your eyes on the skies for kites and other hawks as the miracle of migration unfolds right before your eyes, both in spring and fall. As shared earlier in the chapter about Chuck-will's-widows, the Muse doesn't say, "Sit down and write." She says, "Stand here a minute; I have something to show you." This time she sent her simple message via two curious joggers and a phone call: "Go outside and look up." ๑

Knock, Knock!

A loud "pik" and a descending, horselike whinny direct my attention to an elm tree in my front yard. A small black and white woodpecker is clinging to the tree trunk just above the wooden shelf I placed on the side of the tree a few days earlier. Her tail feathers touch the shelf, making her look as if she is standing on the tip of her tail. She contorts her body first to one side and then the other, grabbing a peanut from the shelf. Then, turning to face the trunk, she pounds away at her prize. After finishing one peanut she turns to pick up another, then another. This is the first time I have seen her at the shelf. Apparently, she has just discovered the bonanza I placed on the tree for the woodpeckers in my yard.

The bird gobbling down the peanuts was a female Downy Woodpecker (*Picoides pubescens*). One of the best known and smallest of North America's woodpeckers, the downy averages six and three-quarters inches in length. The only difference between the male and female downy is the red patch on the back of the male's head. The broad white stripe down the middle of its back separates the downy from all other woodpeckers in North America except the hairy (*Picoides villosus*). The two are almost identical in appearance, but the downy generally has dark bars or spots on its white outer tail feathers and is about two and one-half inches smaller than the hairy. Even though they look similar, they are not closely related. The downy is closer to the western Ladder-backed Woodpecker (*Picoides scalaris*).

The Downy Woodpecker's year-round range extends from southern Alaska across Canada and most of the contiguous United States to the Gulf Coast and into Florida. It is mostly absent from the Southwest, where it may appear locally only in winter. Since its range is so expansive and the bird is confiding and friendly, it is easy to attract this woodpecker to your backyard.

"Found a peanut, found a peanut, found a peanut ju-ust now!" Remember that old song we sang as kids? I could imagine my downy singing the tune when she found one of her favorite foods on that shelf in my front yard. In addition to peanuts, downies have an affinity for other nutmeats, including coconut. They also favor doughnuts, cornbread, sunflower seed, cracked corn, suet cakes, and American cheese. One of their all-time favorite foods is a mixture of cornmeal, lard, and peanut butter. You can offer this treat in the holes of a hanging log or in a mesh bag. Upon discovering the fruitcake I put in the wire basket for the mocker, the downy kept coming back for more. Between the downy and the mocker, most of my leftover Christmas fruitcake was gone by the end of January.

Downy Woodpeckers are attracted to the fruit of serviceberry and wild strawberry plants, to dogwood, mountain ashes, and Virginia creeper. Much to the delight of gardeners, downies also eat beetles, spiders, and snails. Downies are versatile as far as feeders are concerned. In addition to the shelf feeder, hanging log, and wire basket already mentioned, they readily come to bird tables, trays, and small hanging feeders. I see the downy frequently at a vinyl-coated wire mesh tubular feeder that I keep filled with peanuts.

Once you start feeding Downy Woodpeckers you had better remember to keep the food coming or the birds will let you know about it. John V. Dennis tells about a downy in New England that reminded homeowners their feeders were empty by tapping on the shingles on the side of the house to get their attention.

The downies in your backyard may find a dead limb suitable for excavating a cavity eight to ten inches deep. There they will lay their eggs and raise their young. It may be from five to forty feet from the ground. Sometimes they accept nesting boxes. The floor should be four inches by four inches with an entrance hole measuring one and one-quarter inches in diameter placed seven inches above the floor. Line the bottom of the box with wood chips—the downy's only preferred nesting material. The wood for the box should be treated with a nontoxic wood preservative and the box placed out of direct sunlight and shielded from heavy rain.

If you don't like the looks of artificial birdhouses in your yard and you have no dead tree limbs, you can create backyard nesting and feeding trees by anchoring a dead snag in concrete. Either way, natural cavity or nest box, you may be privileged to see some of the courtship behavior and parenting skills of these interesting birds. Once my friend Barbara Garland and I were enchanted as we watched a pair of Downy Woodpeckers from the time the first surface was broken for the entry hole on a pecan tree limb until, two months later, a storm knocked down the dead limb, which contained three nestlings.

As so often happens in the world of nature, we don't always have "happily-ever-after" endings. However, a few days after the storm the downies appeared in the pecan tree with one fully feathered fledgling. Because the downies had the resilience inherent in most birds, we were not too surprised that at least part of this little family survived the storm. Yet had it not been for an abundant supply of peanuts and suet cakes, we might never have had the chance to watch one of nature's dramas unfold right in our own backyard. ⧫

Tying Some on for the Birds

When I was growing up in Arkansas, my family spent many pleasant evenings listening to the radio. One of our favorite programs was *Duffy's Tavern*. It always opened with the proprietor answering the telephone with this dialogue: "This is Duffy's Tavern, where the elite meet to eat!" After we started feeding birds in the early 1970s we dubbed our yard, "Osborne's Tavern, where the elite of the bird world meet to eat." We maintain a dozen or so feeders and three birdbaths throughout the year on our relatively small suburban lot in a residential neighborhood. Some feeders are in the front yard, where I can see them from my "writing window," and some are in the backyard for easy viewing from our dining room.

Mike's illustration of me "tying some on."

Twenty-something years ago I compared bird clientele notes with a friend who lives a block down the street. I was envious when I discovered that Bobby had hordes of American Goldfinches coming to her feeders and I had none. Upon learning that she put thistle (nyjer) seed in special finch feeders, I tried the same for three weeks with no luck. I called Bobby and suggested there must be something else in her yard that I didn't have in mine. After thoughtfully pondering my predicament she said, "Well, I do have two sycamore trees, and the goldfinches love the seed balls on those trees."

I knew it would take years to grow sycamore trees, and I didn't have that kind of patience. I wanted goldfinches, and I wanted them now! I told Bobby I would try to transform our mimosa tree into a sycamore tree, to which she dubiously replied, "Well, I've always thought that only God could make a tree." However, when she saw my determination she helped me clip from her trees several branches that were heavily laden with seed balls. I hurried home with the treasure.

If the neighbors didn't already know I was a bird nut, this surely convinced them of it. There I was, for all to see, precariously perched on a ladder, tying sycamore balls to the winter-bare branches of the mimosa tree above the thistle feeder! I watched the baited branches with bated breath. My insane efforts paid off on the third day when two American Goldfinches found the seed balls and then the thistle feeder. The next day and the next and the next, more and more finches appeared until I was feeding fifty to a hundred goldfinches every day. From daylight until late afternoon goldfinches were everywhere, eating us out of house and thistle. Every available perch was occupied and birds were waiting in line for their turn at the little black seeds. I added two more feeders.

One day when there was absolutely no more room at the inn, suddenly, in the midst of all those gold feathers I saw "red" at the nearby sunflower feeder. A male Northern Cardinal had dropped in to dine. At the same instant, a goldfinch spotted "Big Red." To my amazement, the frustrated yet enterprising goldfinch simply grabbed onto the cardinal's tail and waited for its turn at the coveted food supply. The goldfinch was actually hanging upside down from the end of the cardinal's tail! The dignified cardinal, refusing to be perturbed, kept his cool. He continued eating sunflower seeds as if nothing out of the ordinary was happening.

I know it sounds crazy, but ever since that long ago fall, the ritual has become an annual event at our house. Come the middle of November, I "tie some on for the birds." Our mimosa tree has long since died, so now I tie the sycamore balls to the tops of the feeders. Then we wait for the return of our favorite winter guests. So far, the goldfinches have not disappointed us. I recently learned that if you tie a yellow ribbon at the top of the thistle feeder, the goldfinches will see it and think it's another goldfinch. So now my "tying some on" ritual includes not only sycamore seed balls but yellow bows as well.

Witnessing the unfolding miracle of American Goldfinches as they exchange their olive-drab winter plumage for the brilliant canary-yellow garb of spring makes all the zaniness worthwhile. We are sad in early May when the call of the wild lures the goldfinches to northern regions of the country for their breeding season. Nonetheless, we always hold in our hearts the assurance that our yard in Central Texas will once again become "Osborne's Tavern, where the avian elite meet to eat," if I but continue my ritual of "tying some on for the birds!" §⤚

Travelers from the Far North

When most of us hear the word *sparrow,* we think only of the House Sparrow, that prolific little brown bird that crowds around our feeders all year round, eating us out of house and home. You may be surprised to know that *National Geographic*'s *Field Guide to the Birds of North America* (fourth edition) has eighteen pages of birds with "sparrow" in their names. Many of them spend their winters in our part of the country and may be enticed to feeding stations. Three of my favorites are the Harris's, White-crowned, and White-throated Sparrows.

I consider the large Harris's Sparrow—which measures seven and one-half inches from the tip of its pink bill to the tip of its tail—one of the most handsome of our winter visitors with its black crown, face, and bib. As sparrows go, Harris's has a rather limited winter range. From Central Texas it covers a narrow swath northward through Oklahoma, Kansas, Nebraska, and southern South Dakota. A rare to casual winter visitor in the rest of North America, this distinctive sparrow migrates in spring to nest in the stunted boreal forests of the Far North.

Harris's Sparrow is fairly common within its winter range, especially along hedgerows and open woodlands and brush lands. If you live near its preferred habitat, you may be lucky enough to see this sparrow in your yard. I live one block from an area that used to be wooded. Before it was developed for housing, I saw Harris's Sparrows in my backyard every winter. They came to my birdbath and preferred smaller seeds such as millet that spilled to the ground from post-mounted feeders. Now that large homes have replaced the woods, I no longer see Harris's unless I drive into the country. I miss having them as neighbors.

The immaculate White-crowned Sparrow is distinctively marked. My husband says its boldly patterned, black-and-white-striped crown resembles a football helmet. The white-crowned is a popular garden bird throughout its range, which includes three-fourths of the United States and the Far North into Alaska. High on its list of favorite foods are sunflower seeds, white millet, chicken scratch, peanut hearts, and other nutmeats. White-crowns are well-mannered ground-feeders, somewhat aloof from the rest of the dining crowd, with a dignified, regal bearing.

The White-throated Sparrow's head pattern is similar to that of the white-crowned. However, its broad white eyebrow has a bright yellow spot in front of the eye. Its conspicuous and strongly outlined white throat distinguishes it from the white-crowned.

The White-throated Sparrow is one of the most common winter feeder birds in the South and East. Arriving at feeding stations early in the morning, some may remain until well after dark, feeding mostly on the ground. White-throats are model guests. The presence of other birds does not seem to bother them and they don't bother other birds. They feed like chickens, jumping forward and scratching backward through the seeds with their feet. White-throats prefer small seeds, particularly millet, but they also like finely cracked corn and suet.

Unlike most other songbirds, which are silent from the end of one breeding season to the beginning of the next, these three sparrows are quite vocal throughout the winter.

In case you are unsuccessful in attracting these charmers to feeders located within their range, drive down almost any country road with thick, brushy hedgerows. The three species are known to hang out together. As soon as you see movement, stop, look, and listen for the soft, melancholy strains of "Poor Sam Peabody, Peabody, Peabody"—a short version of the White-throated Sparrow's song. Listen, too, for the Harris's series of long, clear, quavering whistles and the white-crowned's haunting, thin whistled notes followed by a twittering trill.

When you see them, count yourself privileged indeed to catch a glimpse of these travelers from the Far North. ❧

Up Close and Personal

If you maintain a bird feeding station in the summer you may get to observe nesting behavior "up close and personal" in your own yard. A few years ago, while I was writing *The Cardinal* (University of Texas Press, 1992), a pair of Northern Cardinals in my yard repeatedly investigated the nandina bush outside my office window. I assumed they were considering it as a possible nesting site. I kept hoping they would nest there so I could give a firsthand account of their activities in my book. But it was not to be. Not yet anyway.

As luck would have it, the cardinals decided to build in the nandina bush *after* the book went to press. I discovered the female sitting on the completed nest the day after I returned from a birding tour and had no idea how long she had been there.

Why, I wondered, couldn't this have happened while I was writing the book? The first time the female left the nest I got a stool to stand on so I could look into the nest through the window. I saw three eggs in it and for the next few days watched a small miracle unfold inches from my window.

Cardinals are very attentive parents. I soon learned there was a pattern to their behavior. Before leaving the nest, for whatever reason, the female always sang a brief song and made a bubbly, gurgling sound the like of which I had never heard before. I finally figured it out: it was a signal to her mate that she was leaving and it was his turn to take over. He always appeared right after she departed and resumed nest duties until she returned a short time later.

A few days after I discovered the nest, the chicks hatched, filling it with three ungainly bundles with thin pink skin tightly drawn over tiny skeletons and sparsely covered with mouse-gray natal down. For the next twelve days, both parents busily filled hungry mouths that were lined with bright red, making them easy targets for the parents to see in the dark of the nest. The nestlings' main diet for the first few days consisted of insects: moths, bugs, larvae of various kinds, then green caterpillars, and later still, grasshoppers and beetles. A study by ornithologist A. C. Bent reveals that each cardinal nestling is fed an average of eighty-nine times per day. With that kind of service from dedicated parents, the young soon go on a growing spurt unequalled in the mammal world.

The nestling's digestive tract is far from perfect, and each feeding stimulates defecation. The parent bringing food waits on the rim of the nest for the nestling to defecate, then reaches inside and removes the fecal sac—a tough mucous membrane enclosing the young nestling's feces—with its bill. The parent carries the small white sac, which resembles a disposable diaper, far away from the site so as not to reveal the nest's location to predators.

Cardinals have numerous enemies: raccoons, snakes, rats, domestic cats, dogs, and, of course, other birds, such as hawks, crows, and owls. Defending their young from predators consumes a great deal of the parents' time and energy. After the nestlings outside my window hatched, I saw a Blue Jay land in the nandina bush one day while the male cardinal was on duty. The jay seemed curious about the nest's contents, but the cardinal wasted no time chasing him off. Another time, a Carolina Wren landed inches from the nest and began singing its loud "teakettle, teakettle, teakettle" song. There was a sudden flash of crimson feathers as the father cardinal materialized and quickly dispatched the unwelcome intruder.

When I went outside to replenish the sunflower seeds one morning the male cardinal followed my every move with a watchful eye and emitted several loud "chinks." I'm sure he was warning me not to get too near the nest. I'm equally sure he did not know that I was daily keeping tabs on him and his family from my office window.

Naturalist John Burroughs wrote, "Infancy . . . is hedged about by many perils; but the infancy of birds is cradled and pillowed in peril." With all the adversities they face, it is a wonder any of their young ever survive. But survive these babies did! Two of them at least: I never knew what happened, but at some point the third nestling simply disappeared.

Fifteen days after I discovered it, two "almost fledglings" teetered on the nest's rim, exercising and stretching their tiny wings. Perilously swaying back and forth, they tested their strength. Miraculously, they did not fall.

A few days later I watched the parents coax the fledglings from the nest to the outer edges of the bush, then lower and lower until they were on the ground. From my window I was able to thoroughly enjoy their "coming-out party" as the adults loudly urged their babies to follow them. One or the other of the parents would take a few steps toward one fledgling, utter several "chinks," then turn and hop away. If the baby refused to move, the adult repeated the procedure until the youngster made an effort to move toward the parent.

After several moments of urging, the fledglings, by turn, spread their tiny, feathered wings and feebly flew a short distance, landing in a nearby hedge. Each time one of the youngsters made an advance, the parents appeared to praise it with lavish "chinks." Gradually, the parents led their offspring from the side of my house to the thicket in the backyard, where they fed and protected them until the fledglings were independent creatures. I did not see them again until they were almost the size of the parents and coming to the feeders on their own. Had I not been providing food for birds for many years, I might have missed the drama that was unfolding in my own backyard. ❧

Scissorbird Circus

Before us, near the small oak tree in the backyard, the curtain goes up on one of the most fascinating acts in nature's infinitely varied circus. Two of my friends, Barbara Garland and Ethel Noll, watch with me from ringside seats on the patio as the show begins under the Texas sky, the biggest "big top" of them all!

A few moments after we were seated, a pair of Scissor-tailed Flycatchers that had built a nest in the young live oak in Ethel's backyard arrived in center ring. Three young nestlings were waiting to be fed. From her perch on a neighbor's garage, the female flew to the nest tree with a bug in her bill, perched on the topmost limb, and looked around.

"Get ready!" I whispered to Barbara, who had set up her camera and tripod to capture the event on film. "I think she's about to feed the babies." There was, however, a surprise in store for us. As if he had been waiting for the proper cue, the male scissortail, resting on the TV antenna towering above the garage, suddenly darted out and launched into a magnificent aerial display above the female. With loud calls and chattering, he climbed high above her head, stopped momentarily in midair, spread his wings and tail to their limits, and plunged earthward in what seemed to be a suicidal dive. A split-second before he would have been dashed to smithereens, he flared his wings, swerved upward and once again made a death-defying dive. He repeated this kamikaze act several times while the female looked on, still holding the bug in her bill. It was a marvelous spectacle. All that was missing from the scene was a big brass band.

After watching the male's brilliant aerobatic performance, the female finally went to the nest and fed the nestlings. His turn in center ring completed, the male resumed his lookout from the TV antenna. It seemed that his superb "sky dance" was performed solely for the entertainment of the female and, as a bonus, for the audience of three humans as well.

Oklahoma's state bird, the Scissor-tailed Flycatcher is a member of the family Tyrannidae, meaning monarch, lord, or ruler. The "tyrant" flycatchers are so named for their pugnacity in defending their nesting territories. Often you may see them in hot pursuit of a large bird of prey or a crow that threatens their eggs or young. More than once I have seen a scissortail fearlessly attack a Red-tailed Hawk, a Crested Caracara, or an American Crow.

Legend has it that these combative little flyers sometimes alight on the backs of predators and do all the harm they can by savagely stabbing with their bills. Perhaps this type of behavior is the basis of ancient Mexican folklore expressing the theory that the scissortail's favorite food is the brains of other birds. In reality, its favorite foods are grasshoppers and crickets, with other insects that are harmful to crops not far behind. Where the bird is abundant, the Scissor-tailed Flycatcher is an economic boon. Farmers regard this "Texas Bird of Paradise" as definitely one of the "good guys."

The bird catches its prey in a beak equipped with a hook on the upper mandible. Touch-sensitive rictal bristles, whisker-like feathers located around the base of the bill, aid in funneling insects into the bird's wide gape.

Scissor-tailed Flycatchers are among the most picturesque and graceful birds in North America. With wings and tail spread wide, the salmon-pink underwings accented with scarlet axillaries (armpits) are striking in the sunlight. The male's bright shoulder patch appears blood red against the pale gray of his wings. Long, flowing black-and-white tail feathers open and close in flight like a pair of scissors in the hands of a tailor. The bird gets its common name from this action.

The female has most of the same color markings as the male, but her finery is a little duller than his, shaded more toward soft peach than salmon-pink. The male has a reddish crown spot that is usually concealed. He uses this patch of color in courtship displays and to intimidate other males. The adult male's tail is about one-third longer than that of the adult female. According to the age of the male, his tail may be up to nine inches long. The longer the tail, the older the bird. When you see a scissortail with an extremely long tail, you can be sure he's a granddaddy. With a shorter tail, the female is a bit smaller overall than the male. The two average between eleven and fifteen inches in length, including the tail, making them the longest North American flycatchers. In fact, no other North American songbird has such a proportionately long tail. An agile bird, the scissortail is able to turn so sharply it almost seems to pivot on its long tail. Sometimes it interrupts a slow, decorous, straight-line flight by suddenly darting upward.

From mid-March until October or November, scissortails may be found on their breeding grounds, which include most of Texas, northwestern Louisiana, western Arkansas, southwestern Missouri, Kansas, and a small corner of southeastern New Mexico. A good place to look for them is on utility wires alongside roads and highways. I often see them in the city at intersections around traffic lights.

As we watched the scissorbird circus, Ethel told us about the morning she and her husband Bud were awakened by a terrible ruckus outside their bedroom window. Parting the drapes, they saw a pair of Scissor-tailed Flycatchers that seemed to be fighting. The Nolls soon realized, however, that instead of fighting the two were apparently trying to decide where to build their nest. Like the "textbook scissortail" that builds its nest anywhere from seven to thirty feet above the ground and usually chooses a small tree for the nest site, this pair did not depart from the norm. They chose a young live oak tree about eight feet tall, with a trunk no more than six inches in diameter.

All that day and the next, Ethel and Bud observed the flycatchers as they brought twig after twig to the crotch of a branch in the oak tree, scarcely five feet from the ground. Both birds carried nesting materials to the tree, but the female did the construction. After she arranged the twigs into a loose, cuplike structure, both flycatchers gathered bits of fluffy down from the cottonwood trees in the woods two hundred yards from the house. They piled the downy tufts into a ball at one side of the nest and the female later worked each tiny bit into the twiggy lining with her bill.

While the female worked, the male went into a series of rapidly executed ascents and dives. The dramatic effect of such a performance is heightened by the opening and closing of the long, flowing tail feathers, accompanied by a series of loud, chattering calls. The male sometimes ascends to a height of about a hundred feet, drops a fourth of the way to the ground, and then turns sharply on a zigzag course like a roller coaster in its maddening up and down gyrations. Sometimes the bird literally turns backward somersaults on its invisible trapeze. As we soon learned, the male repeats this sky dance frequently throughout the nesting process.

After completing the nest, the female laid four spotted, creamy-white eggs over a period of four days, an average clutch for the species. When she completed the clutch, the female began her twelve- to thirteen-day vigil. Throughout the incubation period, the male entertained the female several times a day with his lovely aerial ballet. Three nestlings successfully hatched on the twelfth and thirteenth days. Later, one of the parents disposed of an egg that was apparently infertile, carrying it far away from the nest site.

Ethel told us the newly hatched altricial nestlings (born helpless and without feathers) looked like small wads of bubblegum, their pink, rubbery skin tightly drawn over tiny skeletons without a hint of down. However, by the ripe old age of five days the nestlings were covered with grayish-white downy feathers. Nine days later the three were fully feathered. Two weeks after the third chick hatched, all three youngsters perched on the edge of the nest as if ready to take a giant leap into the great unknown. Sure enough, later that day the nest was empty.

Ethel began a methodical search of her small backyard, looking under the nesting tree, in the grass along the wooden fence, through all the plants in her flower garden, but with no luck. Finally, she noticed a tiny silhouette on the limb of a small shrub at the end of her flowerbed, a chick crouching silently in the cover of a thorny yaupon holly bush.

Ethel made a mad dash for the phone to call Barbara and me. We couldn't go immediately, but when we arrived two hours later, the baby scissortail was still crouching in its hiding place. The other two chicks were nowhere to be seen. Again we took our seats at center ring and waited to see what would happen next. The father scissortail suddenly climbed his invisible sky ladder high above the yaupon. At the zenith of his ascent he stopped abruptly. Hovering with outstretched wings and tail and loudly chattering, he plunged to within inches of the shrub before climbing back to lofty heights once again. It seemed that he was trying to coax the chick out of the shrub.

After a while, the stunned chick got the message. In weak, fluttering flight, it struggled to the safety of a grassy field fifteen feet away. A few minutes later, the other two chicks appeared across the road and flew as best they could to join the first chick in the grassy field. The parents observed all this action from the TV antenna and we three from Ethel's yard. Occasionally, the parents flew to within inches of where the chicks were hiding, as if offering encouraging words for what was apparently their offsprings' first flying lesson.

It is hard to imagine, but by late October, when hundreds of scissortails gather in preparation for migration to their winter home in Mexico and Central America, these young birds will be skilled flyers and navigators. By then they will have forked tails only a little shorter than their parents' tails. It is even harder to imagine that by next spring, when the three young scissortails return to their breeding range, their tails will be almost as long as their parents'. By that time the youngsters will be aerobatic stars in their own right. Then the Scissorbird Circus will begin all over again. Reserve your ringside seats now. ᔭ

Blue Jays

Love 'em or Hate 'em

I reached for a book, and when I turned back toward my writing window a Blue Jay was feasting at the sunflower feeder. "Wow!" escaped my lips even though I see Blue Jays almost every day of my life. The striking blue, white, and black plumage continues to wow me every time I see a Blue Jay, and its crest adds a regal finishing touch.

Cyanocitta cristata (blue chattering bird with a crest) is one of the most colorful and best known of the corvids. Its range covers two-thirds of the eastern United States and from southern Canada to Mexico. Although seen throughout the year, some local populations of Blue Jays migrate south in the winter and are replaced by birds from farther north. During winter, some Blue Jays venture as far west as Washington and New Mexico. Blue Jays, in the family Corvidae along with crows, ravens, and other jays, travel in large, loose flocks in spring and fall.

It is easy to attract this handsome, raucous blue beauty to your backyard, for the Blue Jay is omnivorous, eating almost anything from insects to fruits, nuts, grains, and even the eggs or young of other species. A tubular wire-mesh feeder with raw peanuts hangs in my front yard next to a log with holes filled with suet mix. One day a Blue Jay was obviously trying to figure out how to get to the peanuts since there were no perches on either feeder. First it clung to the wire feeder with no success. Then it flutter-hovered in front of the feeder with less success. It really wanted a peanut! Finally it landed on top of the log feeder, turned almost upside down and managed to extract one peanut. The jay must have surmised that one peanut was not worth all that effort, because I never saw it there again. From that day on I put peanuts in a bowl on the shelf feeder attached to the tree trunk.

Not only are corvids said to be the most intelligent of birds; they are also some of the most playful. Blue Jays seem to make a game of retrieving peanuts from the bowl. Almost every day, groups of up to four jays come to my feeders, one after the other, as if playing follow-the-leader.

While the others perch nearby, a jay flies to the shelf, grabs as many as nine peanuts at a time (I counted them), and races away. Then another and another comes to snatch its share of the loot.

American Crows, White-winged Doves, woodpeckers, and squirrels also love peanuts and give the jays a little competition. Interesting behavior often happens around the delectable goobers. If Red-bellied Woodpeckers or White-winged Doves are already dining at the bowl when the Blue Jays arrive, the jays perch in the tree and politely wait their turn at the goodies instead of barging in on someone else's party.

I often wonder where they take the peanuts. Do they hide them in some secret cache for future meals? Do they bury them in the ground? Do they stash them in holes in trees for times of hardship during winter? Can they remember later where they hid them? The answer to all these questions is "yes." Blue Jays are known to be good foresters. Acorns and beechnuts are some of their favorite foods. Often they bury acorns that sprout. While squirrels get major credit for burying acorns, Blue Jays may be far more important in replanting oak forests than squirrels ever were.

Remembering that in Costa Rica the Central American birds love rice, one morning I mixed some leftover brown rice with suet mix, raisins, and peanuts. It looked good enough to eat, even to me. I put the new mixture on the shelf to see who would buy. As I might have expected, Blue Jays were the first customers. The first jay took two peanuts. The second came and went so fast I was unable to see what it took. The third and fourth jays gobbled down mouthfuls of rice. The next one grabbed five peanuts before flying away.

Because of the Blue Jay's notorious habit of nest-robbing, some people think they are mean-spirited birds and really don't like to see them in their yards. Even though they rob other nests, Blue Jays are fiercely defensive of their own nests and young. They often dive-bomb other birds, cats, dogs, and humans who get too close to their nests.

I had been watching a Blue Jay nest in my front yard from the time the eggs were laid until the babies hatched. One day I heard Blue Jays putting up an awful ruckus and ran outside to find an American Crow snatching one of the nestlings in its claws, about to make off with it. When I threw open the door, the crow dropped the chick and flew away. I picked up the infant, still half-clothed in down, and placed it back in its nest. The Blue Jays had fallen victims to a member of their own family, Corvidae. The jays apparently are one step down from crows in the food chain.

Blue Jays are as polite about taking turns bathing as they are at the feeding table. One day a flurry of activity outside the dining room window caught my attention. It was bath time for the House Sparrows. They hopped into the birdbath, five at a time. Three different shifts of sparrows came to bathe. They splashed so furiously I didn't think there would be a drop of water left. When the sparrows finished, a Northern Mockingbird zoomed in. A Blue Jay waited patiently inside the hedge while the sparrows and mocker dipped and splashed. When the jay finally got to the bath it finished quickly and found a perch in full sun. It sat there for a long time, soaking up some rays while it preened and dried its feathers.

You don't need a fancy, expensive birdbath to entice Blue Jays to your yard. Any old mud puddle will do. One Saturday night someone forgot to turn off the sprinkler system in our church playground. When the children arrived for Sunday School the next morning, the whole area was flooded—not a fit place for children to play in their Sunday best. The Blue Jays, however, had a heyday! One jay claimed the pool that had collected under the monkey bars as its own private spa. From the tree nearby it plopped into the muddy water, spread its wings, and splattered water in every direction. Then it flew to the monkey bars, shook all over, and preened. Again and again it dropped into the puddle. Each time it went back to the monkey bars to tend its feathers, another jay staked out the puddle under the swing set as its playground. The Blue Jays were obviously having a good time while the children stood outside the fence and watched.

A young boy, watching the show, asked if the birds were males or females. I answered, "I'm not quite sure, because the males and females look alike." The best way to tell Blue Jays apart is to see them during courtship and nesting season. During mate feeding, the male approaches the female with food. He also feeds her while she incubates the eggs.

The Blue Jay is known for its harsh voice. Some people who dislike Blue Jays call them the neighborhood bullies because they are so noisy and boisterous. Loud calls of "Jay, Jay, Jay!" often frighten other birds away from the feeders. A perfectly ordinary Blue Jay may suddenly scream like a hawk or "caw" like a crow. Its mimicry of other birds, especially its imitation of Red-shouldered Hawks, has fooled me on more occasions than I care to admit.

Sometimes Blue Jays are alarmists and warn other birds when danger approaches. I can always tell when an accipiter (a bird-eating hawk) is in the neighborhood by the Blue Jay's urgent calls. The birds know to scatter for cover when they hear that particular cry. Whenever you hear a flock of Blue Jays screaming, check it out. They may be mobbing an owl or some other predator. You may not know it, but the Blue Jay also has a charming, soft and low song that is seldom heard except during nesting season.

Although the Blue Jay is eminently visible because of its large size (eleven to twelve and one-half inches) and vibrant colors, it is an artist of camouflage. It can "disappear" behind a winter-bare branch quicker than you can say *Cyanocitta cristata.*

You may dislike Blue Jays with a passion because of their brash, bold behavior and their nest-robbing habits; or you may thoroughly enjoy watching these intelligent, colorful, playful clowns of the bird world. Blue Jays. Either you love 'em or you hate 'em. I happen to love 'em. ᔒ

Nonpareil

Who could ever forget their first sighting of a Painted Bunting, showiest of all the buntings? The first year I was a birder (1975) two of my mentors, Jean Schwetman and Lorene Davidson, invited me to go along with them when they conducted a Breeding Bird Survey (BBS), using the same route they had followed for many years. Knowing that the Painted Bunting was my most-wanted bird, they practically guaranteed I would see one that day. That was how they enticed me to get out of bed way before the crack of dawn to go.

The beginning point of the twenty-five-mile survey route was sixty miles from Waco. In order to arrive there the required thirty minutes before sunrise, we had to leave home at an ungodly hour. I don't think I slept ten minutes that night because I was so excited about the prospects of seeing the bird of my dreams. About halfway through the route, Jean and Lorene announced we were about to enter PB territory, so I sat on the edge of my seat in anticipation. Suddenly, there was a blaze of color. It was a male Painted Bunting pecking at grit on the edge of the gravel road. It was so bright and beautiful I couldn't believe the bird was real. It seemed more like an escaped cage bird than a bird in the wild. For me, it was love at first sight.

The mature male Painted Bunting (*Passerina ciris*) has a purplish-blue head, lemon-lime back, dark wings and tail, a reddish-purple rump, and blazing scarlet underparts and eye ring. It is truly a rainbow of a bird. Males attain this dazzling attire in their second year. The female is the only *Passerina* bunting that is yellowish-green all over.

Once I made a "bird talk" for some hearing-impaired children and showed them museum specimens of Northern Cardinals, Blue Jays, hummingbirds, owls, and many other birds. When I picked up a male Painted Bunting specimen, and, through an interpreter, told the children its name, a gasp of awe swept over the group. A boy about ten years old signed a question to me: "Did you paint it?" I signed back, "No, God painted it." Then I told the boys and girls about an ancient American Indian legend that tells the story of the day the Great Spirit gave all the birds their colors. Running short of dye, he gave the very last bird, a Painted Bunting, a coat of many colors like Joseph's from the dabs of paint he had left over.

The late Roger Tory Peterson, guru of many North American birders, field guide author, and bird artist, called Painted Bunting "the most gaudily colored of North American songbirds." In the Deep South it is called nonpareil, meaning that it is without an equal in the bird world. Other names by which it is known are Mexican canary, painted finch, rainbow bird, and mariposa, the butterfly.

A few years after my first sighting of this fabulous bird, I was sitting near the dining-room window working on decorations for a women's luncheon when I would much rather have been birding. Looking up from my project I saw six male Painted and four male Indigo Buntings on the ground beneath the window. I had never seen buntings in my yard before, much less a colorful mix such as this. They stayed for several days, adding flashes of brightness to the scene in my backyard.

Perhaps you've guessed by now that *Passerina ciris* is my favorite bird. In the 1980s, when I was leading birding tours, we used citizen's band (CB) radios to communicate between the vans. My "handle" was "The Painted Bunting." Today, some of my older birding buddies who were on those tours still call me by that name, and a hand-painted leather Painted Bunting pin adorns the front of my birding hat.

Painted Buntings have two geographically separated breeding populations. The western population is found primarily in Kansas, Oklahoma, Texas, Arkansas, and Louisiana. The eastern population is limited to the coastal portions of North and South Carolina, and as far south as central Florida. Some scientists believe these two populations comprise two distinct species, although there is no geographical variation in plumage. They winter from Louisiana and Florida to Central America and the Caribbean. The females arrive on their breeding grounds a few days after the males, at which time the males vie to attract the female of their choice through plumage displays and vocalizations.

In their first year of life, males are similar to females and can be distinguished from females only in the hand or when observed singing. Females of the species do not sing. The Painted Bunting's song is a sweet, high-pitched, bright, tinkling sound, a rapid series of varied musical phrases. When the male first arrives on his breeding grounds, he usually sings from perches concealed within the foliage of a tree or bush. Upon hearing its distinctive song, you know the bird is somewhere near, and aware of its unbelievably bright plumage, you wonder why you can't see him. Finally, he pops to the top of the tree, throws his head back and pours out his tinkling notes.

Their preferred breeding habitat contains thickets, hedgerows, and gardens. After they are paired, both sexes search the foliage for a suitable nest site, which includes vegetation strong enough to support the nest, several singing perches for the male, and an adequate feeding ground—usually a grassy field with scattered shrubs. Once they decide on the site, it takes only two days for the female to construct the neat, thin-walled, deep-cup nest in thick foliage, usually in a crotch three to six feet above the ground, but it can be as high as ten to twelve feet. She uses dried grasses, twigs, rootlets, bark, caterpillar silk, weed stalks, and leaves. She lines the center with animal hair, dried grasses, and, occasionally, dried snakeskins.

The female incubates three to four bluish-white eggs speckled with brown. During incubation, she feeds herself at midmorning, late afternoon, and in the evening just before sundown. The female remains on the nest overnight. After the chicks hatch, the female is the sole provider of food for the nestlings for eight or nine days, until they fledge. The male then takes over the care and feeding of the young for about three weeks while the female starts another brood. Sometimes you may see fledglings at your feeders with their parents.

Painted Buntings readily come to feeding stations for sunflower seeds, mixed birdseed, peanut hearts, cracked corn, bread crumbs, suet, scratch feed, and especially white millet. They will return if they find your feeders to their liking. Author John V. Dennis says that Painted Buntings have patronized some of the same feeding stations in Florida for over thirty years.

Painted Buntings will feed on the ground, but they are partial to raised-platform feeders. They like it best when a feeder is filled only with white millet. They sit for minutes at a time, filling their craws with the tiny seeds, giving you ample time to enjoy their dazzling beauty. Painted Buntings bathe frequently to keep their brilliant plumage in tip-top condition, so it pays to have a birdbath in your backyard. They prefer low birdbaths, shallow pools, and the edges of streams. I often see them splashing in shallow water at the edge of the Frio River.

On a mystical, magical spring morning in Central Texas, Harold, Sam, and I were birding along a road near Waco when we came upon a sight none of us will ever forget. A hundred or more Indigo and Painted Buntings, all males, methodically made their way across a weedy field under the cover of a misty rain. The birds landed on the weed stems, riding them to the ground where they ate the seeds from the stalks. We watched in awe until the razzle-dazzle travelers disappeared over the horizon. Is it worth the effort you may have to expend to attract these raving beauties to your backyard? You bet it is! It's like the difference between black-and-white and color TV. ᔥ

Butterfly Garden to Miracle in a Jar

I can't seem to stay out of the backyard these days, and I've fallen head over heels into lepidopterology. Oh, it's nothing like poison ivy, nor is it a deadly disease. Heaven help me! I've gotten into butterflies. Since 1975 I had thought ornithology, the study of birds, was enough. Granted, I had dabbled in astronomy, mammology, and botany, but now these jewels of the insect world have me under their spell.

My butterfly craze started in Concan in the spring of 2000. An influx of butterflies I had never noticed before aroused my curiosity, and I began looking them up in a field guide, which was my first symptom. Then, the next October, our extended family met in Concan for a weekend and we found hundreds of Monarch butterflies roosting in the bald cypress trees by the Frio River, like Christmas ornaments dangling one above the other along the branches.

The incidents in Concan inspired us to do something to attract these beautiful creatures to our yard. We have lived in the same house in Waco since 1963, and until 2001 had never seen the need to do anything to improve the backyard. While our sons Mike, Van, and Sam were growing up, it was a place for tree houses and bag swings. It served as a touch football field, a place to play "catch" with their dad or croquet, badminton, and Frisbee, and a romping place with dogs and puppies. When Sam was a boy, our next-door neighbor, Dick Atwood, taught Sam all about gardening, so he had a vegetable garden in the backyard. After Sam allowed his garden to go fallow, we let the yard "do" whatever it wanted to through the years. The only two things I planted were an American beautyberry bush and a mulberry tree for the birds. Birds and squirrels themselves "planted" a number of other trees and shrubs, giving the place a wild look.

We called a landscape designer and told him we wanted to create a haven for butterflies and hummingbirds. David Nealy designed a plan including only native plants that attract a number of butterfly species, hummers, and other birds as well.

Once the landscape crew began working, I sat in the backyard and "supervised" and photographed every step of the way. I told them this would probably be the best-documented piece of work they had ever done. From start to finish, I shot fifteen rolls of film and gave the landscaper a set of the photos for his records.

At my request, the crew installed a split-rail fence along one side of the yard to add a rustic touch of the Hill Country. Along the fence they planted an array of flowers, shrubs, and trees including flame acanthus, Mexican bush sage, tall blue ruellia, buddleia (butterfly bush), coral honeysuckle, Turk's cap, pink salvia, lantana, possumhaw yaupon, pigeon berry, tropical milkweed, and so on, all guaranteed to bring in butterflies and birds by the droves. I dubbed this section of the yard "June's Butterfly Garden."

Since I am a compulsive "lister," I wondered what would be the first butterfly, bird, bee, or wasp on my new "garden list." Less than an hour after all the plants were in the ground, a gulf fritillary landed on a buddleia blossom to feed. Thus began my "backyard butterfly list." The day after the crew finished the flowerbed, I sat in one spot for an hour. I saw a Monarch butterfly on the buddleia, a smaller butterfly and a skipper (yet to be identified), dozens of red admirals, a tiger swallowtail, a bee with pollen-covered head, an orange sulphur, and a black-and-yellow insect on the majestic sage. Our resident mocker perched briefly on the bottom rail of the fence, thus becoming "the first bird to land on the fence."

Watching the metamorphosis of my backyard, I was reminded all over again that there is a spark of the Divine in every living creature. I couldn't wait to see for myself the metamorphosis miracle of a butterfly. I had always wondered: What comes first, the butterfly or the egg? How does a long, slinky caterpillar change into a chrysalis? How does a wet, crumpled bundle emerge from a rough brown chrysalis and unfold into a strong pair of wings?

I didn't have to wonder for long. A few months after my garden was planted, Jean Green discovered I had never observed the changes with my own eyes and brought me everything I needed to witness the miracle: a Mason jar containing two twigs, a caterpillar, and some sprigs of parsley.

After the green caterpillar with black stripes and yellow spots devoured the parsley, it attached a silken pad to the twig, wove a magical cloak around itself, and awaited its metamorphosis.

Sharlande and I watched the chrysalis for days, hoping we would be present the moment the miracle unfolded. Then one day, while we were eating lunch, a subtle movement on the dining-room table caught our attention. Black wings were tenuously opening and closing inside the glass jar. A butterfly was clinging to the twig for dear life. While I grabbed the camera, Sharlande gently lifted out the twig and held it near a bouquet of daisies on the table. The butterfly crawled to one of the daisies, seeming at home on the flower although a little puzzled about life outside the jar. The butterfly didn't know what to do next. Neither did we.

We turned to *The Family Book of Butterflies,* where author Rick Mikula suggests offering sugar water to a newly hatched butterfly. I mixed the solution, soaked a cotton swab, and held it in front of the creature's proboscis, two parallel tubes located on its head between its antennae. The proboscis uncoiled slowly and began to suck the nectar.

After exposing a roll of film, we took the butterfly—flowers and all—to the patio, thinking the swallowtail needed the warmth of the sun. However, we were a little worried that a hungry bird might fly by and snatch this easy prey from right before our eyes.

We coaxed the butterfly from blossom to blossom with the nectar-soaked swab so I could photograph it from all angles. When it began to rain, we put the fragile insect back into the jar and took it in the house. When the shower ended and the sun came out, we looked again. The butterfly was not moving. It was so still we could see every detail of the pattern on its wings. We feared it was dead, so we immediately took it back outside. There, something unexpected happened: The sun warmed the swallowtail's wings and suddenly it was resurrected. It was as if the swallowtail was telling us we couldn't keep a miracle in a jar.

We placed the butterfly on a purple cone-flower and soon its wings came to life, opening and closing slowly. Then we watched in awe as a patch of black dotted with white, orange, and blue floated across the flowered landscape of my butterfly garden. It flew through the garden arch and rose heavenward. I was reminded of a quote Mona Burchette had E-mailed to me the day before: "Butterflies go wherever they please and please wherever they go."

We laughed when Sharlande remembered a cartoon showing two caterpillars walking down a sidewalk with a beautiful butterfly flitting high over their heads. One caterpillar says to the other, "You'll never get ME up in one of those things!"

After spending three hours on a hot July afternoon focusing on one butterfly, Sharlande and I realized that butterfly watching, like birding, has the power to intensely excite and relax you at the same time and that small miracles don't happen only in jars. They occur in our backyards and all around us every day, whether we are aware of them or not. One last thought: Perhaps the miracle is not only in the mystery of a butterfly's metamorphosis or the miraculous growth of a bird from egg to nestling to fledgling to adult in a few short weeks but in our slowing down to see these things happen.

Oh, my! There's a tiny worm swinging at the end of a silk strand. What do they call a person who studies worms? Never mind, forget all those long terms. I'm no scientist; I'm simply a "naturalist" who enjoys exploring her own backyard. ﹅

Travel Is

for the Birds

Travel Is for the Birds

Some people travel to see museums and various historical
  spots.
Some go for scenic grandeur in climes both cold and hot.
Some go for ancient ruins, some for buildings not quite new.
Some see majestic splendor; others, just a view.

Some go to far West Texas to have a look at stars.
There you may witness Venus or see the red on Mars.
Some go to merry London to view Victoria Tower.
Others go there to hear Big Ben at the striking of each hour.

Just give me a birding hotspot, no matter where it is,
so I can watch the lovely birds and study all their jizz.
Give me Lower Klamath Basin with its grebes, avocets, and
  clowns,
or Ramsey Canyon, Arizona, and the hummers with violet
  crowns.

Take me to California to the Head of Bodega Bay,
where I'll watch the little scoters when they come out to play.
Take me to the Florida Keys—away from all the rest—
where I see a pair of Ospreys attending to their nest.

The Keys are the home of the mighty bird they call the Great
    White Heron.
And there a friendly boatman may toss lunch to a hungry
    pelican.
In the Everglades one gets real close to a heron called green-
    backed,
who fishes upside down 'til his gullet is fully packed.

At Mrazek Pond the spoonbills are resplendent in their pink.
And the rare endangered Wood Stork obtains its food and
    drink.
Take me to Aransas where I'll watch the whoopers all day.
Then I'll see a Reddish Egret perform a lovely ballet.

Let me go to little High Island for migration in the spring.
There I'll watch the warblers bathing and listen to them
    sing.
Bolivar Flats is a wondrous place for a multitude of Skim-
    mers.
On Galveston Bay, at sunset, see them skimming for their
    dinners.

Take me to The Valley—along the Rio Grande.
I'll see Altamira Oriole and Brown Jays close at hand.
Show me a flycatcher, kiskadee, with a bright yellow breast,
Green Kingfisher, Green Jay, thrashers, and all the rest.

Share with me a sunrise on the lovely Llano Grande,
where whistling-ducks and pelicans perform their feats so
    grandly.

Take me to Santa Ana for migration in the fall,
and help preserve a Corridor for Wildlife, one and all.

Costa Rica is a magical place. What else can you say?
That's all!
For in very few places in the whole wide world, can you find
Resplendent Quetzal!
Take me back to Kenya. I'd go there again tomorrow
to see the Black-chested Harrier-Eagle in front of
Kilimanjaro.

Yes, I'll travel the wide world over, both near and very far.
I'll go by boat, by plane, by marsh buggy, and even in
my car.
Just promise me avian species galore! Let me put it in other
words.
I'll look at the sights, but for me, henceforth, travel is really
for the birds! §➤

Address Birds

Certain birds are what I call "address birds." When someone asks where to see a Vermilion Flycatcher around Concan in the Texas Hill Country, I can almost tell them the exact tree in which to look. Want to see a Golden-cheeked Warbler? Go to Lost Maples State Natural Area, cross Cann Creek on the steppingstones, walk a hundred yards up the Pond Trail where you will see a sign on the left that says, "Keep Pets on a Leash." Two trees past the sign look at "three o'clock" in the big-tooth maple. Two feet in you will see the golden-cheek tending its juniper-strip nest atop a clump of ball moss.

It's really that simple with some birds, because they are highly predictable. With others, it's not. It took four trips to the Davis Mountains in West Texas to find my first Montezuma Quail, four to Florida before I checked Limpkin and Snail Kite off my list, and an uncounted number of treks to the Rio Grande Valley to catch the gleaming red eyes of a Common Parauque in the flashlight's beam.

On one of my birding tours in the Rio Grande Valley, we checked the Rare Bird Alert (RBA) daily and learned that a Fork-tailed Flycatcher was in the area around Rio Hondo. A tropical species, it's a casual vagrant in Texas and along the Atlantic Coast. The RBA recording gave specific instructions on how to get to the marshy area in which the bird was being seen. I played the tape over and over to make sure I had the directions written down correctly. Frances Hudson was driving the fifteen-passenger van and I was riding shotgun, reading the directions to her.

Two of the tour participants, Carleton Harrell and Ed Gill, were following in their camper. Around and around Rio Hondo we went, at least three times, but we simply could not find the right road on which to turn. The CB radio crackled to life and I heard Carleton's voice calmly ordering me to ask Fran to pull over to the side of the road for a minute. We complied, and Carleton got out of the camper, casually walked over to my side of the van, and without a word reached through the window and took the map out of my hand. When he was back inside the camper, he calmly announced, "We'll lead now!" In no time at all the two guys were able to find the bird's address and everyone on the tour was able to check the sought-after flycatcher off our day's list as a Lifer.

For twenty years I looked for Le Conte's Thrasher on every trip I made to the western United States. It has a limited range in the arid Southwest. On our way to an American Birding Association convention in Park City, Utah, in June, 1996, Harold and I spent a night in Kingman, Arizona. I called an ABA member who lives in Kingman and asked if he knew where we might find Le Conte's Thrasher. Lucky for us, he turned out to be an expert on finding the bird.

He gave me explicit directions to the intersection of Bacobi and Shinarump Roads. He said the best time to be there is just after sunup, because the bird sings at dawn, making it easier to find. He warned me that the hunt would not be easy. These birds nest in early spring, and by mid-June they stop singing and are quite elusive.

We decided to try to find the bird's address the night before. We mistakenly turned north, not south, on Bacobi Road, and instead of finding the thrasher or its location, ended up watching a Lesser Nighthawk hunt for its dinner, which was a wonderful sight, but we really wanted to find that thrasher. We went back to our motel and called the man again. He said South Bacobi is a couple hundred yards down the road from North Bacobi. We simply had not gone far enough before turning.

Daylight comes early in western Arizona in June. We were at Bacobi and Shinarump before 7 A.M. (early for us), and we were surprised to see the sun was already pretty high in the sky. In the distance we heard the raucous calls of a Cactus Wren. Beginning a methodical search on this dusty country road, we inched the car along a few feet at a time, got out, and looked at every wolfberry bush in the desert because our expert said that was the bird's preferred habitat. Le Conte's is a skulky thrasher, pale colored, matching the desert sand. It hardly ever flies. Instead, it runs across the desert floor with its tail cocked high. We knew we must watch for behavior more than anything; we couldn't rely on sound that late in the morning.

Just as I was about to give up, Harold quietly announced that he saw the bird. I looked where he directed, and sure enough, there was the thrasher standing stock still in the shadow of a wolfberry bush. It was too far away for a good look. When I turned to get my scope for a better view, the bird cocked its tail skyward and ran to the next bush, where it disappeared into the shadows. No matter how hard we tried we couldn't find it again, but we knew it was our bird by its behavior—and its address. It was a Lifer for both of us.

Want to see a Le Conte's Thrasher? Drive to Kingman, Arizona; go to the intersection of Bacobi and Shinarump Roads; turn *south* on Bacobi, and then drive until you see a desert full of wolfberry bushes. ⑤

Rare Bird in Texas

"There it is!" someone shouted. With that signal, the man standing next to me, clad in white shirt and tie, softly commanded, "Charge!" As I stepped forward with the rest of the troops, I observed, half to the man and half to myself, "That poor little bird doesn't have a chance." The entire company of twenty birders strung out along the path went charging single-mindedly into the brush as if obeying our "uniformed commander." The object of our mission was to see a Golden-crowned Warbler from the border state of Tamaulipas, Mexico. It had inadvertently strayed across the Rio Grande to a drainage canal in Brownsville, Texas, little knowing that hundreds of curious birders would seek it out on the other side.

Once we had bungled our way through the thick and tangled under-brush, we found ourselves in what seemed like a deep jungle. In reality we were on the muddy banks of a creek, totally surrounded by thick vegetation. There wasn't enough room for all of us on one side of the shallow creek, so half the company deployed to the other side. One fellow, dressed in a jumpsuit, tried to get across the water, catlike, on a fallen log, carefully placing one foot in front of the other. He didn't see that the log was slippery, and just as he was about to make it safely across, one foot slid, throwing him off-balance. He landed (catlike, again) on all fours in the muddy creek bed.

Each of the other birders, armed with binoculars and high expectations, found a somewhat precarious perch and waited. Some were in muck up to their ankles, others with their boots in the murky water. I was seated on the damp ground, desperately trying to keep my new purple boots out of the mud. Barbara Garland, crouching beside me, calmly whispered, "I guess you know, we're right in the middle of a patch of poison ivy." "I know," I whispered back, "but if I can see the bird it will be well worth the price of an itchy rash." Except for these whispered comments and a play-by-play description of the warbler's movements, there was almost complete silence. It reminded me of a farcical World War II movie starring Abbott and Costello in which the troops, entrenched in a muddy foxhole, await the command to fire.

At the right end of the battle line, someone appointed himself as our play-by-play announcer. His stage-whispered running comments went something like this: "The golden-crown is feeding in company with a Black-crested Titmouse and a Ruby-crowned Kinglet. The three are moving right to left along the ridge on the opposite bank. . . . (long pause) . . .They're low in the brush and difficult to see. . . . (another long pause) . . . Don't give up. They're coming your way." Every time I heard a gasp or a loud, "Ohhhhh!" I knew someone along the line had spotted the target.

The young man next to me was casually leaning against a tree as if he could care less if he saw the bird. Wearing a T-shirt with an ecological message printed on it, something about preserving wildlife habitat, he was the only one exhibiting any sense of calm—or any sense at all, for that matter. Appropriately, he was the first one in our echelon to spot the bird. Coolly, he announced, "The warbler is now on the other side of the creek above that man's straw hat." Sure enough, there it was, at eye level for those of us perched in the poison ivy patch. "Yes, I see it," I replied. "At least I think I see it," I conceded, not having a clear view of the bird at all.

The warbler, moving with quick jerks from branch to branch scarcely a foot above the ground, was barely visible. All I could see was a blur of olive-gray and yellow feathers. I could discern no distinguishing marks such as wing bars and eye stripes. Just ahead of the blur I clearly saw the kinglet, complete with wing bars and a crown that flashed red periodically. Bringing up the rear was the titmouse.

By the time the warbler reached the end of the line, everyone had seen it, some better than others. Then the troops began to emerge from the "jungle" one by one, each in varying stages of disarray, the females of the species with hair disheveled and the males with caps askew. All of us were in wilted condition in the humid climate.

"It was a tough battle, folks," someone said, panting, "but we won!" Someone else expressed extreme doubt about any sort of victory, using expletives I would not dare to print here. He must have had the same view of the bird that I had. The catlike fellow had fared the worst. His jumpsuit was covered with mud up to his knees and elbows, and his binoculars had a thick coat of mud as well. I hope they were waterproof. He apparently had been in similar situations before, because he proudly announced, "Don't worry folks, I have a complete change of clothes in the car."

How did we find out about this rare bird in the first place? Through that wonderful invention the RBA: the Rare Bird Alert for the Rio Grande Valley. Months before, I had planned a trip to The Valley for a group of birders from Waco. The day before we left home I called the RBA and recorded the message.

As I played the recording we heard the friendly, rapid-fire voice of Father Tom Pincelli. "Greetings! This is the Rio Grande Audubon Alert for Monday morning, February the ninth. The Golden-crowned Warbler continues to be seen here in Brownsville. The last reported sighting was last Saturday near the junction of 1419 and 511. Once you reach this junction, follow the drainage canal to your right until you see a small dam. Another canal coming in from the right forms a Y. Cross over the canal, which is dry, and follow a small trail along the side of an abandoned orange grove going into the woods. You'll find red yarn tied on some trees, and it is here that the bird is being seen."

Before making that phone call to the RBA, I had never even heard of a Golden-crowned Warbler. I consulted my copy of Roger Tory Peterson's *Field Guide to Mexican Birds* and there read that the bird was "an olive-gray warbler with a crown suggesting that of a Golden-crowned Kinglet, and with dull yellow-green eye stripes. Yellowish underparts. No wing bars." It sounded as if all we needed to look for was a bird like a kinglet without wing bars.

When we arrived at the junction of 1419 and 511, there were several cars but no sign of people, red yarn, an orange grove, or a Y. After several attempts at finding the right path to take us into the mosquito-infested territory, we took another trail along a high bank that skirted the drainage canal. After only a few steps we heard what we thought was an Eastern Screech-Owl. It turned out to be the young businessman in white shirt and tie imitating the owl in hopes of drawing the warbler out into the open.

"Have you seen the golden-crown?" I inquired quietly. The man shook his head negatively and motioned for us to take the only path we had not tried. We soon found the woods, the red yarn, and the birders from the other cars. We were a varied lot: people in their twenties to senior citizens, a woman from California, and a large group from Houston. The "owl" was the only one from Brownsville. My group of seven from Waco, all seasoned birders, rounded out the troops.

Although I shall long remember "The Golden-crown Caper," as it came to be called by the Waco group, I can't say that I was thrilled with the sighting or the way in which we pursued this rare bird. During our foray, the bird's habitat just about got the best of twenty intrepid birders, and we got the best of it. Even so, our thoughtless antics did not seem to disturb the warbler, because when I checked the RBA two weeks later, "The Golden-crowned Warbler was still being seen at the junction of 1419 and 511."

In my view, the only thing missing at that junction was a guest register to record the names of those souls hearty enough to brave the perils of the jungle for an obscure view of a tiny warbler from Mexico. Pardon me while I scratch my poison ivy. ᔕ

The Courtly Clown of Laguna Madre

The large white bird leaps wildly about in the water on long, cobalt blue legs. Going ninety to nothing in one direction, it stops so abruptly it almost topples beak first into the water. Recovering its balance, it does an about-face and repeats the maniacal leaps in the opposite direction as if suddenly remembering it left something behind.

The bird's shaggy mane blows helter-skelter with these exaggerated motions, reminding us of the disheveled wig of a clown. The wildly flapping outstretched wings look as if they are about to detach from the bird's body. A long, sharp pink bill tipped with black resembles a clown's outlandish nose makeup. My husband dubbed the bird "an avian Groucho Marx."

Surprisingly, on one of its abrupt stops, the bird's head darts downward almost quicker than the eye can see, and its bill disappears beneath the water. Soon it reappears with a small fish clasped between its mandibles.

In sharp contrast, after swallowing the fish, the magnificent bird strolls with liquid motions through the shallow water, matching grace with dignity. We can hardly believe our eyes. At this point we think perhaps it's not a drunken and crazed bird after all, for now it manifests the regal bearing of a queen. But wait! Suddenly it seems as if instant replay has activated as the bird goes into its feeding frenzy once again. Faster than it takes to say "*Egretta rufescens,*" the egret changes from courtly clown to stately queen and back to clown again.

To the first-time observer, these comical, overstated motions may suggest the bird is indeed in a drunken craze. However, to the learned birder, it's obviously a white morph Reddish Egret. No other heron or egret feeds in just this way. In reality, the frenzied leaps serve to stir up aquatic prey

lurking beneath the water. Known as "canopy-fishing," the wildly flapping wings are outstretched like an umbrella to cast a shadow on the murky
water, making it easier for the bird to spot its prey. As soon as it does, one
quick jab with that long, sharp bill is all it takes for the egret to catch a
small fish.

Reddish Egret's former Latin name was *Dichromanassa*, meaning two-
colored. It describes not only its two-toned bill, but also the fact that there
are two distinct color forms (or morphs) within the species: dark and white.
The color is not related to age or sex as one might think. A Reddish Egret
is either dark or white for life. When seen at a distance, the white form
may be mistaken for a Snowy Egret or an immature Little Blue Heron. But
just let it go into its feeding frenzy and there is no doubt about its identity.

In a breeding colony one may see both color forms nesting side-by-
side, and young of both colors may come from the same nest. The sexes
of each form are alike, but the female is slightly smaller than the male.
The two forms are known to interbreed as well, thus producing "calico"
offspring. Spectacular displays of circular and pursuit flights occur during courtship. On the ground, the pair's greeting ceremony consists of
head tosses, touching of bills, and bill clappering and snapping. Once the
female chooses her mate, the male mounts her back and copulation oc-
curs. Mating from time to time while the female is sitting on the nest
further strengthens the pair's bond.

According to the dictionary, "courtly" describes something suitable for
the court of a sovereign. A "clown" is a comic performer who wears an
outlandish costume and make-up and entertains by pantomiming ac-
tions in exaggerated or ridiculous fashion. On the entire checklist of North
American birds, in my opinion, Reddish Egret best measures up to these
definitions. There is no doubt that its comical feeding behavior offers entertainment fit for the highest of sovereigns.

If you wish to see the "Courtly Clown" north of the Mexican border,
go to the Gulf Coast from the southern tip of Texas to the Florida Keys
during any time of the year. The white form is much less common than
the dark. My husband and I were lucky enough to see this comical bird
from The Laguna Madre Nature Trail, a boardwalk at the convention center
on South Padre Island, Texas, one January day. After the show we made
an abrupt stop at Blackbeard's Restaurant on the island, where we didn't

have to do maniacal leaps or wild wing flapping to stir up a superb sea-food dinner. ֍

The Boreal Owl of Cameron Pass

Excitement swept through the banquet room like the "wave" at a college football game. The president of the American Birding Association had just announced that a Boreal Owl was found nesting high in the Rocky Mountains near Cameron Pass. Seldom seen south of the boreal forest, this scarce, elusive owl is near the top of almost every birder's "want list." And here it was nesting near Fort Collins in northern Colorado, where Harold and I were attending the ABA's biennial convention.

After the crowd of six hundred quieted down the president said, "All who wish to see this owl may sign up tonight for an early-morning field trip tomorrow. The buses will depart from the parking lot in front of the hotel at 5 A.M." Nothing short of pandemonium broke out as the crowd of eager birders scrambled for the sign-up sheets.

Later that evening we heard that four buses would transport the two hundred people who had signed up for the event. I wondered how so many enthusiastic birders could possibly "sneak" close enough to one small owl, scarcely ten inches tall, without scaring it half to death.

When we assembled at the buses the next morning, the leaders gave us the rules of the game. Upon arrival at the nest site, everyone would be required to walk single-file up the trail to the owl's tree so as not to destroy the tundra. No one was to make a sound while approaching or leaving the site. No tripods. No flash pictures. No talking or whispering.

The two-hour bus trip seemed endless. Our spirits were high and our sense of anticipation was almost to the point of mania as we tried to suppress our hopes of seeing the much-wanted owl. No one disembarked until all four buses were in place. When given the go-ahead, two hundred people moved silently out of the buses, across the creek, and up the trail to a spot three hundred yards from the parking lot.

Surprisingly, the birders lined up in orderly fashion, short people in front, taller ones in the rear. When everyone was in place with binoculars raised and focused on the cavity twenty feet up the side of the tree, the forest ranger, who had spent the entire previous night guarding the hole from predators, walked over and gently scratched the tree trunk. The owl's head popped into view as if the ranger had sprung the lid on a child's "Jack-in-the-box."

The tiny owl peered straight down to see what had dared scratch on her tree. There, to her surprise, she discovered four hundred glassy eyes focused on her comical face. Her head slowly turned 180 degrees as her bright yellow eyes scanned the crowd from one side to the other. After apparently deciding we were no threat, she vanished into the tree cavity as quickly as she had appeared.

The show was over in less than a minute, but the silent expressions of awe on the faces of the birders told the story. It was as though an unseen hand had drawn back a curtain and, for the briefest moment, the spectators had been part of a rare and beautiful experience.

Although it was difficult to suppress our jubilation, no one made a sound as we retraced our steps down the trail, across the creek, and onto the buses—where the celebration finally began. The crowd of birders let out a cheer for the Boreal Owl that was likely heard in northern Alaska. Since the announcement in the banquet room the night before, we had run the gamut from whispers of restrained excitement to shouts of expectations fulfilled. I knew the sight would be with me for the rest of my life, imperfectly remembered perhaps, yet always within. I had seen the Boreal Owl. ᔅᕽ

Thanksgiving Day in Tierra del Fuego

Every year in late November, I am reminded of the most unusual Thanksgiving I have ever experienced. When I started birding in 1975, I dreamed of going to places where I could see penguins and albatrosses, never thinking my dream would ever come true. But it did when Martin Reid, tour guide extraordinaire, offered to take me and a group of birders from Fort Worth, Texas, on a tour of Chile in November, 1993. In three weeks we covered the twenty-eight hundred miles from Tierra del Fuego, a cold and remote volcanic "Land of Fire," to the Atacama Desert, the driest place on Earth, plus an eight-hundred-mile round-trip to the Juan Fernàndez Islands. Within that long, skinny country, we traversed thirty-eight degrees in latitude and saw dramatic changes in landscapes, habitats, and birds.

After four days of birding by bus around the countryside surrounding Santiago, we flew from Puerto Montt to Punta Arenas at the foot of the Andes on the western side of the Strait of Magellan. It was the most spectacular flight of my life. The magnificent snow-covered Andes on one side of the plane and fjords and glaciers descending to the ocean on the other side were enthralling. I shot two rolls of film through the airplane's windows.

When we came out of the terminal at Punta Arenas, our first bird was a Rufous-backed Negrito, a small black bird with a cinnamon-colored back. Founded in 1848 as a military garrison and penal settlement, Punta Arenas has a population of about a hundred thousand.

On our way from the airport to our hotel we passed a stretch of the Strait where we saw South American Terns and our first Chilean Skua, a stout-bodied predatory seabird. Soon we were in a grassland area where Upland Geese foraged with Southern Rheas, large birds resembling the Ostrich. Other birds of note that afternoon were the Rufous-chested Dotterel, Two-banded Plover, Magellanic Oystercatcher, Magellanic Snipe, Chilean Flamingo, Crested Duck, and Flightless Steamer-Duck.

Two Magellanic Penguin colonies reside near Punta Arenas. We visited the one on Seno Otway. After a brief orientation, we walked a quarter of a mile to a beach where penguins were loafing on the rocks. It was hard to believe I was almost at the southernmost tip of South America, camera in hand, with some of the birds of my dreams less than a hundred yards away. The photo opportunities were far from ideal on that cloudy day, however. The wind was relentless and I had left my tripod on the bus, but I couldn't pass up this chance of a lifetime. Finding a fencepost on which to steady my camera, I fired away.

While I photographed penguins, Martin Reid scanned the sea and soon had an albatross in his sites. A Black-browed Albatross wheeled and turned above the silvery surface of the sea without so much as a flap of those long, sturdy wings—just as I had described their flight to school children so many times back home in Waco. Standing in one spot, within fifteen minutes I saw two of my most-wanted birds for this trip.

The next morning, a ferry took us to Tierra del Fuego. Luckily, Martin is a fantastic spotter and highly skilled at identifying seabirds at an incredible distance from a boat that was far from steady in the swell. During the two-and-one-quarter-hour crossing we saw Southern Fulmar, Dolphin Gull, King Cormorant, Blue-eyed Shag, and Diving Petrel—all new to our trip list. We would have missed them had it not been for Martin's impeccable skill. When the ferry landed, Abhay Annello and I, like two little girls holding hands, were the first of our group to set foot on Tierra del Fuego. We checked into the Hotel Los Flamincos in Porvenir. For most travelers, Porvenir is merely a stopover en route to or from Ushuaia on the Argentine side of the "land of fire." For us Texans it was the gateway to birding in the land of our dreams.

The main thing I remember about my first night in Tierra del Fuego was the fierce wind, howling like a hurricane, waking me at 1:30 A.M. Shutters were banging, shingles on the roof were wildly flapping, and I thought surely the top of the hotel was about to fly away. Soon I was a firm believer that this is the windiest place on Earth, as advertised in the trip brochure. By sunup the wind had died down to a bearable gale.

Thousands of miles from home on Thanksgiving Day, I thought about my family and tried to imagine the aroma of baked turkey, dressing, and candied sweet potatoes wafting through the house. It was impossible for them to imagine what I was doing, riding around this strange barren land at "the uttermost part of the earth." Tierra del Fuego consists of rolling hills, grasslands, virtually treeless landscapes, short scrubby bushes, a few scattered small lakes, dusty roads, extraordinary birds, and far in the distance but never out of sight, the mystical snow-capped peaks of the Andes. It was a singular Thanksgiving Day that I shall long remember. §➥

Birding with Robinson Crusoe

The cloud-enshrouded peaks looked foreboding from my seat in the twin-engine, nine-passenger airplane. A volcanic island with extraordinarily rugged topography was all I saw below. When I was convinced there was no safe place for the pilot to land, a red dirt landing strip miraculously appeared beneath the clouds. It was barely long enough for the plane to cruise to a stop before toppling into the blue waters of the Pacific Ocean two hundred feet below.

The landing was a real heart-stopper for his passengers but routine stuff for our skipper, who makes the flight several times a week. We were glad we hadn't seen the wreck of a small plane near the runway until after we landed. The pilot delivers mail to the island and takes back to the mainland boxes packed with clawless lobsters called Langostas—the main source of income for most islanders. Once in a great while he has passengers such as our group of five Texas birders and one retired rocket scientist, Ernie Franzgrote, who was working on a book about all of the hummingbirds in the world.

We traveled to this remote island to see its special birds. Only nine species of indigenous land birds inhabit the Juan Fernández Islands. Two of the nine are hummingbirds: the Green-backed Firecrown (*Sephanoides sephanoides*), found all along the Chilean coast; and the Juan Fernández Firecrown (*Sephanoides fernándensis*), found nowhere else on Earth but this one group of islands. We had seen the Green-backed Firecrown on the mainland, and I decided I would be happy if the Juan Fernández Firecrown was the only bird I saw on the island. As for me, a chance to see a unique hummingbird was reason enough for this epic journey of a lifetime.

Seeing another endemic, the Juan Fernández Tit-Tyrant, seemed a little more iffy than our chances for the hummingbird. The Tit-Tyrant normally dwells in forests on wooded slopes, mainly in the undergrowth and woodland edges, while the Juan Fernández Firecrown favors the flower gardens in villages.

Tiny, isolated Isla Robinson Crusoe is one of three small islands comprising the Juan Fernández Archipelago in the South Pacific Ocean. The islands are both a national park and an international biosphere reserve. Like many oceanic islands, the national park is a storehouse of rare plants and (to a lesser degree) rare animals, evolved in isolation and adapted to very special environmental niches.

Geologically, the archipelago is a group of emergent peaks from a submarine mountain range known as the Juan Fernández Ridge. The adjacent sea floor around the islands drops to more than thirteen thousand feet below sea level on all sides.

Located four hundred miles from Chile's central mainland, Isla Robinson Crusoe is the only inhabited island in the group. Alexander Selkirk, a Scottish mariner, was marooned there in 1704. He remained in isolation on the island for four years and four months. Daniel Defoe patterned his novel *Robinson Crusoe* after Selkirk's experiences. We were gratified to discover firsthand there really was a "Robinson Crusoe." However, much to our disappointment, we learned there was no "Man Friday" in Selkirk's true adventure. Formerly called Masatierra (far from land), the island was renamed in 1966 in honor of Defoe's novel.

After we landed on the unlikely airstrip, the first bird we saw was a Feral Pigeon (Rock Dove). We decided these doves must be everywhere in the world, even on a remote island in the Pacific Ocean. We loaded our luggage into an ancient blue Jeep. Our pilot, who doubled as our Jeep driver, skillfully maneuvered through the hairpin turns on the frighteningly precipitous one-lane road to Bahia del Padré far below. Thank goodness the Jeep was one of only two cars on the island; it meant we didn't have to worry about oncoming traffic.

A motor launch (fishing boat) with a crew of two was waiting at the dock to take us on the one hour and forty-five minute ride to Bahia Cumberland, halfway around the island's awesome volcanic coastal escarpments. Even though we were about to challenge the largest ocean in the world in a boat that seemed the size of a matchbox, this was one of my favorite parts of the trip. As we glided across the blue water, we caught glimpses of the endemic and endangered Juan Fernández Fur Seals playing in the water and snoozing on the rocks.

We were awestruck by the fascinating geological formations along the way. As we skimmed over the water's surface, stupendous volcanic cliffs towered overhead. One cliff had "streamers" down the sides, which the geologist in the group explained were "dikes": streams of lava that had hardened as they shot up out of the center of the volcano when it erupted thousands of years ago. The water was calm near the shoreline, so we had a pleasant ride. Along the way we passed the place where Selkirk is said to have lived. His cave was hidden by a grove of trees, and it was intriguing to imagine what it must have been like to live in isolation on this island for more than four years.

Isla Robinson Crusoe is about nine miles long and less than five miles wide. Its highest point is Cerro El Yunque (The Anvil), which hovers above the village of San Juan Bautista, our destination. With a growing sense of anticipation and adventure, we arrived at the dock in Bahia Cumberland where we saw a sign that read: "*Bienvenido a Chile y a Isla Robinson Crusoe: Poblacion 600 habitantes.*" We disembarked from the fishing boat, grabbed our luggage, and walked the 150 yards to Villa Green, the lodge that served as our home for the next four days.

Soon after we settled into our cozy rooms, Martin Reid, our tour director, knocked on everyone's door and announced that a male Juan Fernández Firecrown was in a tree behind our lodge. We rushed out for our first look at this splendid hummingbird.

The male has been described as brick red, rich cinnamon-red, cinnamon-rufous, or incandescent copper—a stunning contrast to the green female of the species. The male's wings and tail are very dark, almost black. He has a dazzling, iridescent, fiery-orange crown. We couldn't believe our good fortune. Thirty-five minutes after landing at the dock, we logged our first "target bird" on the island, the main reason I had come to this exotic out-of-the-way land.

Unlike the hummingbirds we were accustomed to seeing in the states, the Juan Fernández Firecrown has enormous feet in proportion to its five-inch body. Its main source of nectar is a plant commonly known as the "cabbage tree" that grows only on this island. Its large yellow blossoms hang downward. To obtain nectar, the hummer clings to the cabbage tree blossom with its big feet, hangs upside down, and pokes its slender bill into the throat of the blossom.

The Juan Fernández Firecrown is critically endangered due to predation by introduced cats, European rabbits, and coatimundis; by deforestation; and by introduced plants. Sadly, the hummer's population has dropped so alarmingly in the last decade and a half that we may very well have been among the last outsiders to see this remarkable hummingbird. Not many tourists (or birders) visit this isolated place.

For dinner the first night we had huge portions of Langosta, all cracked open and ready for us to dig out. At every meal except breakfast we had some form of lobster. I thought I had died and gone to heaven, or at the very least to the Garden of Eden. Isla Robinson Crusoe is touted as one of the most tranquil places in all of Chile. The relaxed pace of life there became evident to us very quickly. It was easy to fall into the pattern of the laid-back islanders. I went to bed the first night knowing we were in a very special place. It was truly Paradise Found.

We had two full days to explore this peaceful island on our own, a perfect wind-down from the frantic traveling of the past two weeks on the mainland. Our tour had taken us from one end of mainland Chile to the other—all twenty-eight hundred miles—from the driest place on Earth, the Atacama Desert in the north, to cold and windy Tierra del Fuego in the south. We had seen 263 species of birds, 203 being Lifers for me. Along the way we had ridden in eleven airplanes, thirteen buses, five boats, two vans, one pickup truck, one dump truck, one taxi, one sedan, and finally the ancient blue Jeep. We were ready for some slow-paced birding.

When we walked out the front door of our lodge on the first morning, a Juan Fernández Tit-Tyrant proved much easier to find than we had anticipated. The shaggy-headed bird was perched in a tree right above our heads, as if waiting to be added to our list. It is a funny looking ash-gray little bird with white streaks and a scraggly black crest, making it look as if it is having a bad hair day.

The entire village of San Juan Bautista is built on the mountain slope. One morning I went for a walk on my own. To avoid getting wet during one of the island's frequent rain showers, I ducked into a small chapel about halfway up the mountain. The sanctuary, with basic but comfortable furnishings, was about the size of our master bedroom back home, maybe twelve by fifteen feet. The base of the communion table was a large tree trunk. The table was graced with an exquisitely embroidered white tablecloth. There were eight simple wooden pews with kneeling rails. A large poster of Santa Teresa hung on the wall, and lace curtains covered the two small windows. I was able to enjoy a few quiet moments of solitude in this unexpected sanctuary while waiting out the brief shower.

That afternoon I had long photo sessions with the male and female Juan Fernández Firecrown in the garden behind our lodge. It was a good opportunity to study the striking differences between the sexes at close range. The female is beautiful, but she is so different from the male that for years the male and female Jaun Fernández Firecrowns were thought to be separate species. She has slate-colored wings, a glittering turquoise-green back and rump, and snow-white underparts. The feathers on her throat and flanks are spangled with turquoise-bronze spots. She has an iridescent purplish-blue crown and a metallic blue-green patch at the nape. When I found her, she was all fluffed up and sleeping, seemingly in a state of torpor. Because these hummers are so used to living near people, they are quite confiding and allow close approach even when they are awake.

After finishing my photo session, I walked down to the village square and found a group of young boys playing. All the islanders are very friendly, and the boys began talking to me in their native tongue. They became frustrated when they kept asking me the same question over and over, then realized that I didn't understand what they were saying. Finally, one little boy got right up in my face and asked loudly in English, "What is your name?" We had a good laugh after that, shared names all around, and I took pictures of them. I wished I had taken my Polaroid camera so I could have given them the pictures right there.

All too soon it was time to leave this tranquil place. After bidding farewell to the proprietors of Villa Green, we gathered our luggage and walked to the dock and our waiting motor launch. On our way back to Bahia del Padré we saw Kermadec Petrel soaring and dipping over the blue Pacific waters. The petrel proved to be our last "new bird" of the trip. As we neared the dock, a Juan Fernández Fur Seal escorted us, coming to the side of the boat when we got out to climb the steps to the jetty. The seal poked its head out of the blue water, looked at us, and made a squeaky sound that I interpreted as "*Vaya con dios.*"

Our skipper was waiting for us in the blue Jeep. The ride up the precipitous road back to the landing strip was not nearly as frightening as it had been four days earlier. The plane took off under overcast skies. Fluffy clouds blotted out any view of the ocean most of the way back to the mainland, which was just as well. It gave me an excuse to close my eyes and sleep or dream of the unique hummingbird I had come thousands of miles to see. For me, this once-in-a-lifetime journey was truly a storybook adventure in which, in my childlike imagination, I went birding with Robinson Crusoe. §➤

Photo Session with a Green Heron

The small, chunky bird crept stealthily from between the tall, brown stems of the cattails lining the stream. Pausing motionless, the keen-eyed bird looked all around to see if danger lurked nearby. Satisfied the way was clear, it silently lifted one short leg and then the other, placing its long-toed feet one in front of the other along a limb only inches above the clear water. As it moved, it seemed that not one tiny muscle twitched in its upper body. While birding in Everglades National Park, Barbara Garland and I were thrilled to have such a close encounter with a Green Heron. So dark and camouflaged is its plumage, Barbara and I might have missed it had we not been stealthy and keen-eyed ourselves. At eighteen to twenty-two inches in length, this heron inhabits both freshwater and saltwater marshes, pine and mixed woods, thickets, mangroves, reeds, and cattails.

It is one of the most widely distributed heron species in North America, appearing in the eastern two-thirds of the nation as well as all along the West Coast. The adult bird's shaggy cap is greenish-black. The sides of its head and neck are a deep chestnut, its back dark. In spite of its former name (Green-backed Heron), its back appears more blue than green. Yellow eyes and legs add to this handsome bird's striking appearance.

Barbara set up her camera and tripod as quietly as she could on the Anhinga Trail, scarcely twenty feet away from the bird. She focused the lens and tripped the shutter. The power winder clicked off several shots. When the heron heard the noise he stretched his neck to full height, raised his shaggy crest, jerked his tail, and carefully investigated the camera gear and us from his perch. Dressed in camouflaged clothing, we tried to stand as still as the heron himself, hoping to blend into the environment as well as he did. It must have worked, because after a few moments of intense scrutiny, the heron assumed his hunting stance on the branch, his stare fixed on the water below.

Green Herons feed on a variety of small fish, frogs, crayfish, crickets, snakes, snails, and mice. They employ various hunting techniques to obtain these foods, often wading through shallow water with a halting gait, dragging one foot across the streambed in hopes of stirring up food. Sometimes they stand patiently in a crouched position, seemingly for hours, at the edge of a pond or stream, and when small fish appear they strike with lightning speed. They grasp the fish between their mandibles rather than spearing it with their long pointed bills as some other herons do. Then they throw their heads back sharply and swallow. Sometimes you can watch the movement of the fish as it makes its way down the heron's bulging throat.

Once, at another location, Barbara photographed a Green Heron fishing from atop a small waterfall. He adroitly snatched minnows as they tumbled through the falling water. Green Herons in captivity have been observed using objects such as feathers and food pellets for bait, sweeping them through the water to lure their prey, in much the same manner as a fisherman wielding a fly rod.

The heron in our photo session chose the direct approach for his fishing method. He slowly lowered his head closer and closer to the water's surface. Suddenly he plunged headfirst into the water and remained upside down for several seconds, his feet still clinging to the perch, like a trapeze artist. When he emerged, he shook his head vigorously to sling the water from his feathers. Then he slid his long, shiny tongue along the edge of his bill, as if unwilling to allow even the tiniest morsel to escape his taste buds. The heron repeated this sequence over and over for an hour or more. Each plunge resulted in incredible fishing success.

Patience, persistence, and maintenance are critical to the survival of all the wildlife living in the beautiful but harsh environment of the Everglades. After patience and persistence paid off in the food-finding department, the heron turned to the next duty of the day: maintenance of his feathers. It is essential that birds keep their feathers in perfect condition. One way they do this is by preening. The bird fluffs the feathers on a certain part of its body, takes each feather in its bill and gently bites and strokes it until the barbs are smoothed and locked together again. Meticulously, it probes under the outer feathers to remove dust and parasites. Sometimes while our heron was preening his breast, small tufts of loose down were visible in his bill. He spread first one wing and then the other, twisted his neck until his head was upside down, and peered beneath each wing to see if any parasites or dirt were present.

Continuing his grooming, the heron spread his upper tail feathers, thus exposing an oil gland—the uropygium—at the base of his tail. This gland secretes a substance that prevents the feathers from becoming brittle. Some authorities believe it acts as an antibacterial and fungicidal agent as well. As if dipping a pen in an inkwell, the heron touched the tip of his bill to the gland and transferred the oil to his feathers.

Finished with grooming, the Green Heron turned to walk away. Suddenly he stopped, as if he had just remembered something. Oh, yes. He had almost forgotten. The feathers on his neck and head needed attention, too. Being unable to reach them with his bill, the heron twisted his body like a contortionist until he was able to rub his neck and head back and forth over the oil gland. This final act completed, the heron appeared satisfied with his feather maintenance as well as with his appetite. Our last glimpse of the Green Heron was when he walked back between the stems of cattails through which he had first appeared. Then, as unobtrusively as he had appeared, he vanished into the marsh that is his home. The Green Heron had terminated our photo session. ❧

Who-Cooks-for-YOU-awl?

"First one up, plug in the coffeepot!" This became the rallying cry of one of my family's favorite birding vacations many years ago. It happened in the heart of the Blue Ridge Mountains in the southwestern corner of North Carolina, eight miles south of Brevard. Here you may find your choice of secluded cottages. Some are tucked into the sides of mountains. Some nestle among trees. Others hug the banks of streams, and still others overlook placid lakes. All are surrounded by nature's splendor, providing sanctuary for humans and wildlife alike. We vacationed there twice in the 1980s, both times choosing a cottage called "Roadrunners II," nestled among the trees, an ideal place for our hobby of watching birds. The birds in that area in mid- to late summer are relatively quiet, as is life in those mystical mountains. That is the kind of vacation destination we like: a place that affords solitary walks in the woods, lazy canoe rides, the sounds of gurgling streams, and soft birdsongs typical of the end of nesting season.

Harold was usually the first one up. Almost every morning while we were there he would get up for a walk around the lake long before Sam and I awoke. Twelve-year-old Sam and I thus awakened each morning to the sound of a bubbling coffeepot. By the time Harold returned from his daily walk, Sam and I had cooked sausage and biscuits and packed them into a picnic basket with hot coffee, juice, and jam. Then we would walk to a woodland glen scarcely a hundred yards from our cottage. A short trail led from Turkey Run Road into an eastern rain forest where a rhododendron thicket provided the ceiling for our breakfast chamber. Delicate ferns and wild violets carpeted the spongy floor. Here and there long-stemmed pink flowers poked their heads above the fern tips, and giant hemlocks rose high above the canopy.

One morning, the only sound we heard when we arrived in this enchanting place was a rushing mountain stream. We spoke in whispers, not wanting to disturb the tranquility. A dragonfly with flashing red eyes flitted about over the water, pausing now and then in a flutter of gossamer wings. A spider wove a silver network, row upon row, so intricate of pattern we wondered at its complexity.

Blue Jays broke the silence with loud cries. Were they trying to awaken an Eastern Screech-Owl? No, there was only a small woodpecker wandering through their territory. Why were the jays so upset at a Downy Woodpecker? Then we realized that perhaps they were upset with us because we had lingered so long in their spot. You see, we took small bites and chewed slowly, trying to make our feast of food and surroundings last as long as our feast of seeing.

When it came time to go, the guys went back to the cottage to plan our daily hike while I went in search of birds. One day, the object of my search was a pair of Hooded Warblers that had been reported by a local birder. I took a few steps off the road and entered another enchanted setting. For a few moments I stood silently until my eyes adjusted to the dim light. Then a bird, as much startled by my presence as I was by its sudden movement, sprang from the ground to a low branch. Perhaps because I wanted it to be, I thought it was the female Hooded Warbler. I looked for her small nest near the ground, but if it was there, the crafty bird had succeeded in hiding it from my curious eyes as well as making herself invisible to me.

Suddenly, I heard a noise that sounded like an "Audubon Squeaker," a small wooden device used to attract birds. I searched the shady underbrush until I spotted a female Ovenbird fussily darting from branch to branch about twenty feet away. Her rufous crown was erect, her tail cocked. As soon as I realized I was the source of her agitation, I stepped out of the woods. Her fussing ceased. I never found the Hooded Warbler.

When I arrived back at the cottage I learned that Sam and Harold had chosen "Tanager Trail" for our hike. The trail map they were studying promised sightings of an old still and a waterfall. We hiked the narrow, wooded trail in single file with Harold in the lead. Suddenly, he stopped, pointed, and raised his binoculars. When Sam and I followed suit we saw a male Black-throated Blue Warbler. We clearly saw his black throat, cheeks, and sides, and the steel blue-gray of his upper parts. Then we saw the distinctive "pocket handkerchief," a spot of white barely visible on each of his folded wings. He was a Lifer for all of us, so we were grateful the bird remained long enough for several satisfying looks.

A few minutes later Harold stopped again and pointed out a Pileated Woodpecker, the largest of our woodpeckers. We had heard its loud drumming and calls on numerous occasions during the previous days, but this was the first time we got to see the bird.

After two and a half hours of hiking and viewing birds, waterfalls, and stills, we returned to "Roadrunners II" and ate lunch on our screened porch. A Scarlet Tanager serenaded us, sounding like an American Robin with a sore throat. After lunch we settled down in ringside seats for some lazy animal watching from our living room, which was blessed with large floor-to-ceiling windows. From this vantage point we lounged on the overstuffed couches and pretended we were lying on the soft forest floor with a canopy of trees for our roof and walls.

Chipmunks and squirrels entertained us with their antics on the deck railing where we had placed sunflower seeds and bread for all the wild critters. Among our avian entertainers were: White-breasted Nuthatches that made their entrances headfirst down the tree trunks; Carolina Chickadees and Tufted Titmice that scampered in and out almost too fast for us to see them; Northern Cardinals that enjoyed slow, leisurely meals; gluttonous Blue Jays gobbling seed after seed nonstop; a loud family of American Crows; and an Eastern Towhee that devoured the chunks of bread.

Tantalizing us with incessant calls, but for the most part staying out of sight, were: White-eyed, Red-eyed, Yellow-throated, and Blue-headed

Vireos. Timid Black-and-white Warblers refused our food offerings, as we knew they would, and opted for insects they gleaned as they crept along the branches. A Gray Fox strolled by and circled the house. Our most surprising, and certainly our most unsettling visitor, was an albino skunk. We were careful not to rile him.

When the animal show slowed down a bit, we went for a swim in the junior Olympic pool a mile from our cottage, but a sudden thunderstorm sent us scurrying back home. The heavy downpour created a thousand waterfalls as it rushed down the hills, and thunder rolled through the forest like an invisible gigantic bowling ball. When the storm ended, the trees and flowers glistened in the clean sunlight and the pungent aroma of wet earth and woods filled the air.

After supper we walked down to the mirror-like lake, which softly reflected the trees, mist, and mountains surrounding it. Only an occasional ripple altered the picture as Sam dropped in a hook in hopes of catching a meal-size trout. The fish weren't biting, though, so we went for a canoe ride. Harold taught Sam how to row as the Native Americans did: without making the slightest sound. When the canoe ride ended, we slowly made our way back up the mountain to our cottage and sat on the deck to await the sights and sounds of evening. Leftover raindrops from the afternoon shower dripped in an unsteady rhythm from trees all around us. Wood Thrushes began an antiphonal concert of their loud, liquid song, lasting until dark. From some distant limb in the forest a Barred Owl inquired, "Whooo—whooo—who cooks for you? Who-cooks-for-YOU-awl?" The Eastern Towhee, who had insisted all day that we "Drink our teeeeeeeee!" emphatically answered the owl with, "Tow-heeeeee!"

As the last sliver of daylight slipped over the mountaintop, the flying squirrels appeared as if they had been waiting offstage for the proper cue. They glided from tree to tree, then hopped over to the feeder above the deck and dined elegantly by porch light. As the flutelike notes of the thrushes faded with the light, myriad fireflies began their nightly ballet, flicking their magical lanterns now on, now off, dancing to some inaudible music. Suddenly, the droning of a jet at thirty-nine thousand feet brought us back to reality, reminding us it was time for sleep. Lying in bed with the window blinds wide open we could see dark silhouettes dancing against the moonlit sky, with here and there a twinkling star peeking through. The owl inquired once more, "Whooo—whooo—who cooks for you?" Yawning, I answered, "First one up, plug in the coffeepot!" Then it all began again. ❧

Rock, Rock, Step, Step

In her book *Operating Instructions,* Anne Lamott relates an inspiring story of a blind man running the Dipsea race in California on the arm of his best friend, who could see. Lamott said the race route is grueling, with unbelievably steep uphill and downhill stretches over rugged, rocky terrain. Holding the hand of his blind friend, the seeing man called out every rock, root, and step along the way. They ran joyfully, tripping and falling at times, but making it to the finish line, connected and safe. Lamott said it was the purest statement of faith she had ever seen.

I was reminded of this story when Harold and I were on a 1997 birding tour in Ecuador. Two months before the trip I had finished a grueling race of my own, breast cancer and five months of chemotherapy, so I was not the strongest person in the tour group. Also, one of the men—Jerry, an orthopedic surgeon—had retired from his profession earlier than he had planned because of Parkinson's disease. Each day on our quest for birds, Jerry, taking slow, halting steps, did a much better job of keeping up with the group than I did.

Ecuador is said to have more birds per square mile than any other country in the world. Of the twenty-six hundred species of birds in Latin America, fifteen hundred are found in Ecuador. One day Mitch, our bird guide, announced we would drive to San Rafael National Park to search for one of the most famous of South American birds, Andean Cock-of-the-Rock. It is a foot-long, chunky bird that looks more like a figment of Dr. Seuss's imagination than a real bird. The catch was, it lives in rocky ravines near mountain streams at elevations ranging from sixteen hundred to eight thousand feet in the Andes, and we would have to hike two miles up and down steep, rocky inclines for a chance to see the bird. Unfortunately, Mitch forgot to tell us we would be gone from the bus for two hours or more, so none of us carried any water with us. This proved to be

a huge mistake, since it was one of those long, hot, humid jungle trails—
and rocky and rugged to boot.

With Harold holding my hand every step of the way, I felt like the blind
man running the Dipsea race. About a mile into our hike we came to a
rushing stream that was more like a waterfall than a river. We had to cross
that torrent somehow if we were going to see this strange, mystical bird.
Mitch pointed out the safest place to cross and then he and Dwayne
Longenbaugh stood on a slippery rock on the other side of the stream,
ready to help each person get across safely.

Harold and I were at the back of the line with Jerry in front of us. I
took one look at this rushing river crossing and thought I could go no
farther. I would just have to wait for the others to come back. When Mitch
told me they would not return by the same route, my heart sank. I looked
at Jerry and thought, if he can make it, I can make it. I watched him fearlessly inch his way up the rocky slope. Upon reaching the crossover, his
tiny steps were magically transformed into one giant leap as his right foot
reached tenuously across three feet of raging white water, from one slippery rock to another. With a little help from his friends, Jerry made it
across. With a lot of faith, Harold behind to steady me, and the strong
hands of Dwayne and Mitch to pull me across, I made it, too.

Soon Mitch heard the raucous cries of the bizarre birds we had come
to see. During mating season, male Andean Cocks-of-the-Rock gather at
a "lek," a sort of dance arena high in the treetops, displaying themselves
like cocks to attract the females. Making weird squawking, grunting noises,
they dance and hop about with energetic wing flapping. The females come
to the lek to mate, after which they retire alone nearby to build their cup-
shaped mud nests. They plaster the nests to the sides of damp vertical
rocks with saliva, hence their name: Cock-of-the-Rock.

The Seussian cock has rich orange-red plumage and appears incandescent in his shady home. His bizarre, fan-shaped crest, like a child's
"koosh ball" atop his head, all but hides his small, yellow bill. His wings
and tail are black. The smaller female is chestnut-colored. The species'
distinctive shape makes them unmistakable to identify. But that does not
mean they are easy to see. Despite their large size and intensely colored
plumage, we caught only dappled glimpses of these splendid shy members of the cotinga family as they danced through the treetops. Neverthe-

less, their rare performance made every rock and grueling step of the trek worthwhile. We made it to the finish line, connected and safe. Rock, rock, step, step. 🐦

One-Thousandth Life Bird

It was number one thousand. That may not seem so impressive when you consider the possibility of there being ninety-six hundred in the whole world, but it was *my* one thousandth, and that made it significant to me. This milestone in my birding career could not have happened in a grander place than Amboseli National Park in Kenya, East Africa.

In the summer of 1992 my husband and I accompanied a study group from Baylor University (Waco, Texas) to Kenya. Soon after deciding to go, I purchased a field guide to the birds of East Africa and began to study. This trip was not really a birding tour. However, as you may imagine, I can make any outing into a bird excursion, even if it's only a trip to the grocery store. Never having been to Africa before, the trip was a particular challenge for me. When we left home, my World Life List stood at 855 species. My goal for the trip was to reach, and possibly exceed, one thousand. Allow me to do the math for you: I needed to see at least 145 new species.

We had a two-day layover in London to break up the long, harrowing journey to Kenya. I was so excited on the overnight flight from London to Nairobi that I did not sleep a wink. I spent the entire night restudying the East Africa bird book from cover to cover. I have never studied so hard for anything in my life! We first set foot on African soil in the dark of night at 3:33 A.M. We boarded a bus that would take us to our living quarters on the campus of the Baptist International Conference Center at Brackenhurst, twenty miles outside of Nairobi. The ride to Brackenhurst through the mountains in the half-light of dawn was spectacular. The red radiance on the horizon cast an eerie, rose-pink glow on everything it touched. The dark silhouettes of acacia trees against the rosy sky reminded us of travel pictures out of *National Geographic*. We fully expected a giraffe or an elephant to materialize in the mystical light.

We arrived at Brackenhurst just as the sun came over the horizon. When we stepped off the bus the avian dawn chorus greeting us was overwhelming. The first bird I saw on the continent was the African Pied Wagtail, a relative of our Northern Mockingbird. Our one-bird welcoming committee was singing at the top of his lungs from the rooftop of the administration building.

After settling into their rooms, most people went directly to bed. Not us! We went for a walk around the grounds and discovered a plethora of birds at our binocular tips. Iridescent sunbirds, the flying jewels of Africa and distant cousins to our hummingbirds, were present in large numbers, feeding on the plentiful flowers decorating the grounds. A Hadada Ibis was perched in a poinsettia tree that was taller than my six-foot husband. Two Giant Kingfishers flew over as we explored our new surroundings. An Augur Buzzard hovered high overhead as if suspended on invisible string. A Black Kite soared round and round, and there were weaverbirds that we could not find anywhere in the bird book. My Life List grew by leaps and bounds during the first moments of our stay.

From the edge of the conference grounds located high atop a mountain, our first glimpse of Mount Kilimanjaro, 150 miles away, convinced us that we were indeed in Africa. Every day after arriving in Kenya, two of our traveling companions, Buddy and Tresa Gilchrest from Waco, asked me, "How many new birds today, June?" And each day I gave them the tally. Even though the Gilchrests say they are not serious birders, they told me they wanted to be with me when I saw number one thousand to share in the exhilaration of the moment.

On June 9, two weeks after our arrival in this beguiling country, we went on safari to Amboseli National Park, north of the border of Tanzania, in the shadow of Mount Kilimanjaro. Long before we reached the park entrance we saw our first White-bellied Go-Away Bird (yes, that is really its name), Red-billed Hornbill, and Crested Guineafowl. Giraffes and other wildlife were all along the roadside for close-up views. Red-billed and Yellow-billed Oxpeckers were on the necks of the giraffes eating insects that plague these marvelous animals. Right after entering the park we saw a huge body of water, the result of a recent rainfall. Hundreds of shorebirds were feeding there, and around its perimeter were thousands of Greater and Lesser Flamingos, giving the impression of a delicate pink outline to the shoreline. I was frustrated for three reasons: I did not have my telescope; very few shorebirds were pictured or described in my field guide; and the driver would not stop the van so I could get a better look.

At the end of that fabulous day I needed only five new birds to reach my goal of 1,000. I wrote in my journal, "Tomorrow should be my BIG DAY." June 10 dawned clear and beautiful. Buddy and Tresa rode in the safari van with Harold and me during a prebreakfast game drive. The driver told us that heavy clouds hide massive Mount Kilimanjaro on some days, but the gods were smiling on this special morning. We were blessed with spectacular views.

In rapid succession I ticked off numbers 996, the spectacular Secretary Bird, through 999, the White-headed Vulture, and our excitement mounted. With bated breath we wondered what bird would become number 1,000. We didn't have to wonder long. Suddenly, Tresa said in a quiet voice, "June, there's a large black-and-white bird in the top of an acacia tree. Have you seen that one before?"

When I turned to look, Black-chested Harrier Eagle went down on my Life List as number 1,000. To top it all off, the tree in which the eagle was perched was picturesquely located with Mount Kilimanjaro as a backdrop. How lucky could I get? The four of us snapped picture after picture while I reveled in the moment.

During the course of that five-week African safari (it really wasn't a birding tour, mind you), I identified more than one-fourth of Kenya's 1,200 species of birds, for a grand total of 302. Since then I have added more than 600 additional Lifers to my list on trips to Chile, Costa Rica, Ecuador, and Mexico; but until I reach number 2,000—*if* I reach 2,000—this event will stand out as my most memorable moment in birding.

Take me back to Kenya. I'd go there again tomorrow to see the Black-chested Harrier Eagle in front of Kilimanjaro. §◆

An Unlikely Sanctuary

The sign attached to the chain-link fence caught our eye as we drove past. In large, bold letters the sign proclaimed: "BIRD SANCTUARY." But what we saw as we peeked through the fence certainly did not look like any sanctuary we had ever seen. An odd assortment of boats in various sizes and descriptions and in various states of repair stood propped up on wooden frames within the confines of the fence. Several workmen were busy cleaning, sanding, and applying fresh paint to the boats. A large crane towering over the yard was jockeying a new mast into place on a sailboat.

Standing just outside the entrance to the busy boatyard, Barbara Garland and I stared dubiously at the sign, wondering whether this place could really be a sanctuary. The shrill cry of an Osprey flying overhead suddenly interrupted our pondering. We had both heard the call many times before in areas as different as the lush boreal forest of British Columbia and the place where we presently stood near the aquamarine waters of the Florida Keys. Scanning the skies with our binoculars, we soon spotted the familiar long, crooked wings of the circling Osprey. The bird gripped a large fish tightly in its talons. In typical Osprey fashion, the huge bird kept the fish's head pointed directly into the wind to reduce resistance.

Almost immediately, we heard the call of another Osprey drawing our attention to a massive conglomeration of sticks perched precariously on a makeshift platform on top of a tall lamppost. A female Osprey, bright yellow eyes gleaming, peered over the rim of the large stick nest. When she spotted the male, her eyes followed every tilt and turn of her mate's flight as he circled high above the nest. At that moment, a Bald Eagle appeared out of the blue. The eagle made several dives at the Osprey, attempting to make him drop the fish; but the Osprey would not be deterred from delivering the fish to its intended receiver: his mate back at the nest. After thwarting the eagle's efforts and chasing off a Turkey Vulture and a Red-tailed Hawk as well, the Osprey sailed in for a landing on the pile of sticks that formed its nest. The boatyard was beginning to look more like a sanctuary every minute.

As the Osprey neared the nest, Barbara and I noticed that the fish had no head. Since a fish can live for quite awhile out of water, the male Osprey eats the head to prevent the fish from flopping out of the nest when he places it there for his mate. The fish's head is the male's share of the meal. After landing on the edge of the nest, the male placed the fish next to his mate. She arose from her brooding position, inspected his gift, picked it up with her talons, and flew with it to the top of the mast on a boat anchored in the bay nearby. There she ate what was left of the fish while her mate took his turn on the nest.

Barbara and I were so engrossed in the Osprey drama we were startled to hear a man's voice behind us. "Did you come to see our Ospreys?" "No. Well, yes," I stammered. "You see, my friend and I are here on a birding vacation. We were driving down the Keys looking at birds when we saw your sign and stopped to see what kind of sanctuary this is."

As we exchanged introductions we discovered the man was Dave Westfal, owner of the boatyard. When he invited us in for a closer look, we asked his permission to photograph the birds. As soon as he said it was okay, we set up our cameras and tripods and started clicking off exposures before we realized we needed to be higher than ground level to get a better angle on the nest. When Dave heard us say we needed to be higher, he brought a ladder and asked which boat we thought would give us the best advantage. We looked for the tallest one near the nest and chose the *Scintilla,* a double-decker job. Dave placed the ladder against the side of the boat and we scrambled up. He handed our photography gear up to us and we were in business after we climbed to the upper deck.

Dave was working on the boat next to the *Scintilla,* so we began asking him questions about the Ospreys. It was then we learned that Dave had given the fish hawks a helping hand with their nest. When he first discovered the Ospreys working on their nest several weeks prior to our visit, their chosen site was a few feet away from where we stood atop a boat davit. The davit stood at such an angle that all the nesting materials the large birds placed on it promptly slid off. Adding to the Ospreys' dilemma, the boat's owner had intended to take the boat out periodically during nesting season.

Dave said the persistent birds worked unsuccessfully on that site for several days before he devised a scheme to help them. A lamppost stood near the anchored boat, but it was not as high as the davit, so Dave added an extension to make it equal in height. Then he built a flat, level, plywood platform, providing a firm base for the Osprey nest. There he placed a few large sticks, attempting to attract the Ospreys' attention to the new site.

The birds persisted in trying to use the leaning structure for several days, paying no attention to the level platform and sticks. Realizing that the single-minded birds needed still more help, Dave nailed a broom upside down to the top of the davit, trying to discourage the Ospreys from continuing their futile efforts there. Another two weeks passed, however, before they took the hint and began building their nest on the platform.

Barbara and I were unable to remain in Florida long enough to watch the Ospreys complete their nesting cycle, but Dave kept us informed of their progress. He wrote that people had reported hearing a chirping noise coming from the nest two or three weeks after we were there. They thought it was probably a young Osprey, although they could not see one. When curiosity got the best of Dave, he asked the crane operator at the boatyard to lift him high enough to look down into the nest while both adult birds were absent. All he could see was what appeared to be a brown hairball on one side of the nest.

"No babies!" he reported to the other man as he came down from the crane. However, two or three weeks later, someone saw a young Osprey standing on the edge of the nest, testing its wings. The tiny brown "hairball" Dave had seen earlier was indeed a young Osprey. "Apparently," Dave wrote, "when the parents leave and danger looms, the baby flattens itself in the bottom of the nest, blending in perfectly with its surroundings."

Several weeks later we heard from Dave that the young Osprey was on the wing, learning to catch fish with its parents. It was a hopeful sight. Far too often, human projects cause great harm to wild creatures and ecosystems. It was refreshing to see the positive effect one man's efforts could have on a pair of Ospreys, providing them a second chance at nesting success. ❧

Loon Music and Birding by Canoe

For more than a quarter of a century I have held a special fascination for loons. After seeing my first Common Loon migrating on the Upper Texas Coast during my early days of birding, I knew I would have to go to a place where I could see and hear loons on their breeding grounds. Our friends, John and Gloria Tveten, Texas naturalists and authors, annually spend the month of June at a resort on Leech Lake near Walker, Minnesota. They had told us so many wonderful things about the area, including stories of loons you could get close to by fishing boat or canoe, that we decided it just might be the best place to go.

The Common Loon is the only one of five North American loon species that winters on Texas lakes and along the Gulf Coast. That black-headed, checkerboard-bodied water bird with ruby-red eyes and a strange assortment of calls, is Minnesota's state bird and is found mostly in the northern two-thirds of that state during the spring and summer. So, what better place than the land of ten thousand lakes to try to accomplish my goal? Harold and I made reservations for July 7–14, 2001, sent our deposit to the resort at Leech Lake, and started making plans for a long car trip.

After our arrival, it didn't take long to discover it is a family resort, where people, mostly from surrounding states, go for a week each summer to fill the nine cabins. The week we were there, we were the only couple from as far away as Texas, the only ones there without children, and the only first-time visitors. Some of the families have become such close friends that they make it a point to be at Leech Lake at the same time every year. The resort has a number of amenities for its guests: canoes and fishing boats for rent, volleyball and basketball courts, a pool table in the lodge, a small sandy beach area with a swimming hole, campfires on the beach every night, beach toys, a water trampoline, and paddleboats for the kids.

Shortly after settling into our cabin, Harold and I sat on the deck with a clear view of the lake, anticipating the first sound of loons. Our wait was shorter than we anticipated. After only a few minutes we heard an abbreviated tremolo echoing across the stillness of the lake. From that moment on, our days and nights for the next week were full of loon music.

Once you hear the voice of a loon, you are not likely to forget it or lose the urge to return for more. Loon music is mystical, magical, mythical, mysterious, primordial, primeval, eternal, and evocative. Loon calls may be compared to a baby's wail, the howl of a lone wolf, hysterical laughter, a tremolo, a yodel, or a maniacal scream that sends chills up your spine. Indeed, the varied calls of loons defy description. They are truly "the song of the wild," the symbol of the northern wilderness.

Loons are among the most primitive of avian families. Fossils of the earliest known loon found in England, *Colymboides anglicus,* date from the middle Eocene Epoch, some 50 million years ago. Is it any wonder this mystical bird has captured the imagination of peoples for eons and today lives in legend, myth, and science alike?

Loons may look and sound primitive, but they are highly specialized, ideally suited for swimming and diving. Building their nests near the waterline, they easily slip into the safety of water when threatened. With large webbed feet set far back on their bodies, they are terrestrially challenged. For a loon to take flight, it must patter across the surface, beating the water with both feet and wings, until it is airborne. Once in the air its flight is strong, direct, and graceful.

Having solid rather than hollow bones, the loon's streamlined body is less buoyant than those of other water birds. It is capable of diving to depths of 180 to two hundred feet and remaining submerged for up to fifteen minutes. The position of its legs and feet is ideal for propelling it through the water at a high rate of speed.

Hearing loons every night and day was good, but we wanted more. We wanted to *see* them as well. One evening an Iowan, Steve Burnett from the cabin across the road, invited us to go with him in his fishing boat to look for the loons he had seen earlier that day while fishing. At dusk, as the low-sliding sun cast a golden glow across the lake, we saw the silhouettes of four loons engaged in their nightly ritual of swimming, diving, eating, and calling. In our imagination we were truly "On Golden Pond." One after the other, the Common Loons arched their long necks and thrust their compressed bodies forward, disappearing beneath the surface without leaving a ripple. Who knew where they would resurface? They can swim underwater as far as half a mile.

We toured the lake as long as light allowed. The next morning, again in Steve's boat, we found a pair of loons feeding two offspring. Steve skillfully guided his boat to within twenty feet of the group, turned off the motor, and we sat enraptured while I shot three and a half rolls of film and Harold caught the show on the camcorder. Each of the parents— who, incidentally, mate for life—took turns diving and remained submerged long enough to catch small fish. Resurfacing, they fed first one baby and then the other. When too great a distance separated the adult loons, one would call to the other and they would swim toward each other. At one point, while we sat in awe of the loons, a Bald Eagle suddenly appeared, hovered, and then dove for a fish. Harold and I both captured this on film, too. What a feast of hearing and seeing.

Surrounded by the Great Mystery of this primeval bird, we were totally under the loon's spell. Its lonely call and the aura of its presence soothed our minds and calmed our spirits. The hauntingly beautiful music will forever remain a signature upon our souls, and we shall return for more.

Any lake, indeed, every lake, holds a myriad of secrets—within its depths, on its surface, around its shores. Having toured the lake twice in Steve's motorboat, we wanted to see how it would be to go silently and stealthily. One morning we rented a canoe. We began the adventure with no preconceived notion about the secrets we might discover. We decided to look at everything anew, as if through a child's eyes. As we pulled away from Leech Lake's shore, a group of Northern Pintail ducks swam lazily by. Rowing slowly and as quietly as possible through the river channel connecting Leech Lake and Lake Benedict, we saw a sign that read, "NO WAKE IN RIVER." Was this a command or an announcement? The water was so still that we decided it was an announcement.

We floated silently, becoming one with the water and its surroundings. When we slipped under a highway bridge, Cliff Swallows flew out in all directions. Their juglike nests, made entirely of mud balls, were stuck to the underside of the bridge. Small, feathery heads peeked out of entry holes at the top of each nest, hungry mouths open wide, anticipating the return of their parents with food. An Eastern Phoebe rested on a bridge strut, flicking its tail up and down in typical phoebe fashion.

Birding by canoe turned out to be as much fun for me as "birding by chair" or "birding in a parking lot," especially when someone else is paddling the boat. If nothing else, it is a peaceful way to bird. There is hardly any noise other than the occasional splash of an oar slicing through the water, or the persistent "witchity, witchity, witchity" of a Common Yellowthroat coming from somewhere within the dense stands of cattails along the shore.

While gliding through the water in a canoe, everything seems to move in slow motion: scenery along the shoreline; a river otter swimming by; a bright yellow American Goldfinch hovering at a thistle blossom; dragon-flies flitting here and there, occasionally alighting on a yellow water lily; a Red-winged Blackbird investigating the contents of the lily's petals and calling out "konk-la-ree." Even the sounds seem to play in slow mode. The mournful wail of a Common Loon, from some distant place across the lake, sounded as if the record was about to run down.

On the morning of our canoe adventure, the water's surface was flat-calm, mirror-smooth, reflecting the clouds, the cattails, and the trees along the waterline. The only time the water was disturbed was when a fishing boat passed, sending ripples in its wake. I snapped photos right and left. When I got the pictures back, the mirror images were so perfect it was hard to tell if some of the photos were right side up or upside down. Drifting silently and slowly, watching and listening intently on a lazy morning in July, we discovered a few secrets of beauty on a lake in north-western Minnesota.

Rachel Carson wrote, "Those who contemplate the beauty of the earth find reserves of strength that will endure as long as life lasts." Harold and I recommend listening to loon music in person and birding by canoe as two of the best ways we know of to contemplate the beauty of the Earth. ❧

Enchanting Songster of Mount Rainier

As the Boeing 737 approaches Seattle the pilot announces that Mount Rainier is visible on the left of the plane. Indeed it is; totally unveiled in its grandeur. It is my favorite mountain in the lower forty-eight states. It looks harmless enough, but this majestic symbol of the Pacific Northwest is actually an active volcano encased in thirty-five square miles of ice and snow. Its deeply cut slopes show that its last eruption was a long, long time ago. Born of volcanic fire and shaped by glacial ice, at 14,410 feet, Rainier is the mightiest peak in the Cascade Range, the highest mountain in the "Evergreen State." In these parts, it is often called simply, "The Mountain." In the distance we see Mount Hood at 11,235 feet, and Mount Saint Helens chopped off at the top by its 1980 eruption after more than a century of silence.

When we arrive at our hotel we discover that we can see Mount Rainier from our room. It is rare to see it so clearly. Bright sunny days are few and far between this time of year in Seattle. But once again, the gods are smiling; for three days we have a splendid view.

Sitting at the window, I marvel at the sight. My imagination takes me back a dozen years to our first visit to Mount Rainier National Park. I remember, as if it were yesterday, hearing a sound, tenuous and strange to my ears, the moment I stepped out of the car at Paradise Lodge. It was impossible to tell if it was a bird or some other creature of the montane forest. Trying to find the source of the airy sound that so captivated me, I searched all around in the dimness of the northern twilight. When Harold returned after parking the car, I pointed in the direction from which the sound was coming and asked if he knew what it was. He was just as puzzled as I.

When I had almost given up, I picked out the vague outline of a small bird at the spire of an ancient Douglas fir. Its head thrust back, mouth open wide, throat quivering, the bird was in full song. Again I heard the mysterious vibrations. For the life of me I could not identify the bird in the deepening darkness, even with the help of my ten-by-forty binoculars.

I went to bed that first night with those haunting notes reverberating in my mind. Before giving in to sleep, I read the words of Kevin Zimmer in *The Western Bird Watcher,* where he describes "the ethereal notes of the Varied Thrush" as "the sound of the redwoods." I had read those words time and again while preparing for this trip with the hope of hearing the bird sing. That night I vowed to discover for myself if the "ethereal" sound I heard was the evening song of a Varied Thrush.

Only once before had I seen the handsome, robin-like bird, resplendent in blue, orange, and black plumage, only a fleeting glimpse of a male, with no chance of hearing his enchanting song. Neither could I remember ever hearing a recording of the song of this bird of the Northwest. So, in more ways than one, I was in the dark on my first night in the shadow of Mount Rainier.

The next morning, after breakfast, Harold and I drove around the park, absorbing the scenic splendor. Dominating the landscape at every turn was the majestic mountain. Dominating my mind with every birdsong was the exquisite refrain from the night before. At Inspiration Point, in full view of the mountain, we stopped to read the words naturalist John Muir penned over a hundred years before: "There stood the mountain, wholly unveiled, awful in bulk and majesty, filling all the view like a separate newborn world, yet so fine and beautiful it might well fire the dullest observer to desperate enthusiasm."

I wondered. Muir's description of the mountain seemed to match the mood of my own frantic search for the mystery caroler. In my mind I paraphrased Muir's words: "There sang a bird, filling all my mind like a separate newborn sound, so fine and beautiful it might well fire the dullest listener to desperate enthusiasm." At Louise and Reflection Lakes we heard the organ-like notes again, seeming to come from far away. At the trailhead to "The Bench" overlooking Snow Lake, we decided to hike the trail to see if, by chance, we could track down the elusive songster. As we followed the winding trail, the sky above us was the color of a Mountain Bluebird. Meeting very few other hikers, we felt as if we owned the mountain, the forest, and the day.

We came to a boggy area covered with a boardwalk. Thirty or forty feet from the end of the boardwalk I chanced to see a male Varied Thrush flitting out of the bushes to forage on the ground. I silently signaled for Harold to focus his binoculars on the bird, which seemed not to notice us. We observed the thrush's every move, hoping against hope that it would suddenly burst into song. Silently, I asked, "Are you the bird that invaded my dreams last night?"

Throughout the day, everyplace we went in the park, we heard the ventriloquial strains of the unearthly sound. We left Mount Rainier National Park the next day without knowing the identity of the ghostly singer. However, the next week, at a birder's bed and breakfast in Vancouver, British Columbia, I asked our hostess if she had a recording of the Varied Thrush. She handed me a cassette, which I took with a sense of reverence. As the notes poured from my small recorder, once again in my mind, I was on the slopes of Mount Rainier at twilight, reliving a few magical moments in time. Only now I knew for certain the "enchanting songster of Mount Rainier" was indeed a Varied Thrush. ৯

A Birthday Walk in the Park

The Pacific Northwest is known for its dark, moist, shady forests of giant conifers and an abundance of ferns and other exotic plants. Its wetness makes it unlike any other forest on the continent, a true temperate rainforest. Seattle is blessed with scores of public parks ranging in size from a city block to hundreds of acres, many of them left in their natural state. The Northwest's mild, wet climate permits flowers and other flora to flourish the year round, adding greatly to the beauty of the parks.

In June, 2001, Harold and I flew to Seattle for Sam's graduation from Seattle University's School of Theology and to celebrate my seventieth birthday. June 7 dawned bright and beautiful. While eating breakfast in our hotel room, I looked toward Lake Washington for my first birthday surprise: a Bald Eagle soaring over the lake. Mount Rainier loomed magnificently in the background. I took that as a good omen for the beginning of a new decade in my life.

When we got to Sam and Laura's house that morning, they asked how I wanted to spend the rest of my special day. You guessed it. "I'd rather be birding," I said emphatically. Their backyard is literally six feet wide, dropping dramatically into a steep, wooded ravine at the edge of Carkeek Park, a jewel in Seattle's chain of wild areas. We drove to one of the park entrances and set out on Carkeek's wetland trail along the banks of Piper's Creek, ending on the beach at Puget Sound. The tall trees and thick foliage reminded me of the Big Thicket in East Texas, and birding at Carkeek was just as difficult as in the piney woods. We heard a variety of birds singing, but most of them were so high in the trees it was impossible to see them. As we walked along the path, one persistent song resonated in our ears: three or four short, clear notes followed by a buzz and then a trill. Sam told me it was the Pacific Northwest subspecies of the Song Sparrow, *morphna*. Since I was not familiar with its song, I wanted to see the bird for myself. After several minutes of searching, our efforts paid off. Sam, the first to spot the bird, pointed out a male Song Sparrow perched on a snag at the edge of the dense streamside thicket. The bird sat with its head thrown back, its throat vibrating as the lovely notes filled the air.

Even though I'm familiar with Texas Song Sparrows, the Northwest subspecies looks distinctly different. Not only is their plumage different, it is also difficult to identify Song Sparrows positively by their song alone because they have different dialects in different parts of the country.

Musicians to the core, Song Sparrows are well named. During a typical spring morning, males may sing as many as twenty different melodies, ending the day having improvised nearly a thousand variations on their basic themes. Some writers declare the Song Sparrow to be "the unchallenged virtuoso of the sparrow clan." I am now among those writers. Downstream from the Song Sparrow, I stopped to watch a Common Raven dip a morsel of food into the creek before swallowing it. An American Robin bathed at the water's edge, then flew to a damp branch to preen. American and Northwestern Crows flew noisily in and out of the woods, letting us know in no uncertain terms that we were invading *their* territory.

Earlier in the day, Sharlande had faxed to me seventy wishes for my seventieth birthday. One of the wishes turned out to be prophetic: "70 days when the phone doesn't ring, 70 times when you hear a thrush sing." As we neared the end of the trail, the acoustic signature of the afternoon came from a Swainson's Thrush high in the trees and apparently high on the hillside. Although we never saw it, I was certain of its identity. Its flutelike song spirals upward like the trees it lives in. On numerous occasions through the years, I memorized the distinctive song during spring migration in Waco's Cameron Park, never dreaming that on my seventieth birthday I'd hear it "70 times" on its breeding grounds in the Pacific Northwest. What a beautiful way to end my birthday walk in the park. With Walt Whitman I exulted, "O liquid and free and tender" as the thrush's song spiraled its way to heaven. ᵌ

West Texas Birding

The Davis Mountains in far west Texas are like an oasis in the vast stretches of the Chihuahuan Desert, a green island rising above the surrounding scrubby desert vegetation and rolling grasslands. Davis Mountains State Park is located four miles northwest of Fort Davis, Texas, via

State Highway 118. Its 1,869 acres encompass an unusually scenic portion of Texas.

We have visited the park many times and always stayed at Indian Lodge, styled after southwestern pueblos and nestled into the side of the hills in the park. In 1933, the Civilian Conservation Corps (CCC) built the original portion of the lodge, in which many of the walls are more than eighteen inches thick. Our favorite room is located in this section. The furniture, also built by the "CCC boys," as I remember my father calling them, was fashioned from cedar logs. The chairs are so heavy that it requires a Herculean effort to turn them toward the windows looking out over a scenic panorama. We have spent many hours sitting in those chairs taking in that view. The park is located in the rolling foothills of the Davis Mountains, the most extensive mountain range in Texas. We have to keep reminding ourselves that this is Texas, not Colorado. Since the park is between the desert plains of lower elevations and the piñon juniper-oak woodlands of intermediate elevations, the flora and fauna represent both grasslands and woodlands—habitat for some of the most interesting birds in the American Southwest.

When we visited there in August, 1995, I set up a bird feeding station right outside our door. Keeping it simple, I spread black-oil sunflower seeds on the adobe railing that outlines the walkway around the lodge. I made a birdbath using the lid from the jar in which the seeds came. Soon we had a few familiar bird visitors as well as some we don't see in our part of Texas. One of the most colorful was a male Western Tanager. It has a red head, bright yellow underparts, and a black mantle, wings, and tail. The wings are made more striking by bright yellow wing bars. This male was either molting or immature: his head was splotched with red instead of being solid in color. Western Tanagers winter primarily from central Mexico southward, so this one was probably just about ready to migrate. Another colorful visitor was a male Black-headed Grosbeak, which has a black head and a large triangular-shaped beak—the better to crack open seeds. Its underparts range from cinnamon to orange, with a yellow patch on its belly. Its black wings are marked with wide, white wing bars, and it has a robin-like song. Like the tanager, it migrates to southern Mexico for the winter.

We were looking out the window one day when a dainty, black and yellow Lesser Goldfinch stopped to feed. This tiny four-and-a-half-inch bird is jet-black on top and lemon-yellow underneath. Its white wing bars make him look as if he is wearing a sergeant's chevrons on each wing. A White-winged Dove's nest was in a mesquite tree just outside our door. The mother was still tending her nestlings. She found my food offerings quite convenient. All she had to do when she was hungry was drop to the railing, store a few seeds in her crop, and fly back up to the nest a few feet above the railing.

The familiar birds that came to the all-you-can-eat buffet were House Finches and House Sparrows by the dozens. There was no need to hang a hummingbird feeder. The lodge employees keep several sugar-water feeders going all around the lodge. At one location near the restaurant, Rufous Hummingbirds darted in and out all day, putting on a show that we enjoyed from the porch swing nearby. This feisty little male hummer is reddish-brown almost all over, with an iridescent orange-red gorget (throat patch), and a green cap. The female has a green back and cap and rusty red flanks that contrast sharply with her white belly. Instead of a solid orange-red gorget like his, her throat is speckled with rows of iridescent orange and green spots. These hummers were just passing through on their long and arduous journey to southern Mexico for the winter, some of them possibly having nested as far north as southern Alaska.

One morning when we stepped outside to go to breakfast, a family of Phainopeplas greeted us. In the Silky Flycatcher family, this is one of my favorite West Texas species. Its silhouette is similar to that of a Northern Cardinal. The male is shiny black except for a couple of white patches in his wings that show when he is in flight. He has a crest like a cardinal's and deep red eyes. The female is gray where the male is black. Both have long tails. A juvenile was with them, almost identical to its mother. To me, the call notes of the Phainopepla sound exactly like a human whistling.

In Davis Mountains State Park, the camp hosts often put feed out in a special place behind their mobile home early in the morning and late in the evening. If you are lucky, you may see Montezuma Quails wandering down the mountain for their morning and afternoon treats. This lovely bird was formerly called Harlequin Quail, which to me is a more appropriate name for such a distinctively marked bird. The male's black and white face pattern is like that of a comic character in *commedia dell'arte*. This rare bird is on the endangered species list. As noted earlier, I made four trips to the Davis Mountains before I saw my first Montezuma Quail in 1985. Now that the hosts feed them in the park, they are much easier to see.

On quiet evenings we sat out on the deck and listened for the night sounds. We often heard Great Horned Owls calling to each other on the mountain behind the lodge. One of the eeriest sounds was the call of the Common Poorwill. In the nightjar family and a close cousin to Chuck-will's-widow and Whip-poor-will, this is a bird that one more often hears than sees. Its call is a plaintive whistled, "Poor-will-ip. Poor-will-ip."

If you have never been to Davis Mountains State Park, it is well worth the trip. The scenery is gorgeous and the birds delightful. It is a good birding destination to combine with a trip to Big Bend National Park about a hundred miles to the south. ॐ

Parking-Lot Birding

As I have said before, the Muse comes at odd times and in unexpected places. She usually doesn't say, "sit down and write"; but how many times has she implored me to "Park here a minute, I have something to show you"?

One day, as I pulled into the crowded parking lot of my favorite grocery store in Waco, it struck me that someone should write a "Birder's Guide to Parking Lots." Perhaps that will be the title of my next book. The birds spinning my mind in this direction were two flycatchers I frequently see when I drive down the streets of Waco during the summer. On the wires above the flock of cars was a Scissor-tailed Flycatcher feeding its young. Not far away, two Western Kingbirds did a mating dance in midair. Great-tailed Grackles swaggered around, scavenging food from the pavement. At the bank across the street, a Blue Jay scolded as I drove into the drive-through lane. Almost every parking lot in town has its own Northern Mockingbird. One spring, a pair of mockers set up housekeeping at Lowe's Garden Center in Waco and were seen darting onto the parking lot to catch insects for their young. Their nest was in a potted tree inside the center.

During June and July for the past few years, the best avian show in Waco could be viewed from the Super K-Mart parking lot. Every evening at dusk, thousands of Purple Martins gather in the sparse trees, the "staging area" for martins from all over Central Texas before they migrate to South America. This show usually pulls out of town in late July. During the summer, go to any shopping mall or hospital parking lot across the country after dark and see Common Nighthawks hawking insects around the tall lights. Their loud, nasal "peent" lets you know they are present.

From the parking lot at the First Baptist Church in Hewitt, Texas, I watched a Great Horned Owl and a pair of Red-tailed Hawks raise their young. At KWTX, the CBS affiliate TV station in Waco, a pair of Western Kingbirds dared to nest atop the 220-foot camera tower. After we watched them on the channel's weather segment for several days, the fledglings had a soft landing on the grassy area beside the parking lot from their lofty launch pad.

In the parking area of a picnic spot in Arizona, I saw a nesting pair of Rose-throated Becards. In Miami it was Yellow-winged Parakeets; at the tourist information center in Harlingen, Texas, Red-crowned Parrots. In Mexico, south of the Tropic of Cancer, we stopped at a small roadside restaurant, where, in a tree in the parking lot, we saw a Ferruginous Pygmy-Owl, a species I had chased all over the Rio Grande Valley without success. In Mexico, the owl is known as "*cuatro ojos*" (four eyes) because the two dark patches on the back of its head look like little eyes.

At Montana's Glacier National Park, our target bird was the Blue Grouse. After the park naturalist told us the best place to find the bird, we drove the entire length of Going-to-the-Sun Road. Along the way, we saw a grizzly bear stalking into the woods and thanked our lucky stars we were in the car—but no grouse. When we got back to headquarters, a Blue Grouse ambled across the parking lot and practically got into the car with us. Our "parking-lot bird" at Rocky Mountain National Park was a White-tailed Ptarmigan, normally seen on rocky alpine slopes and in high meadows; at Mount Rainier, a Varied Thrush.

One spring I was guiding a group of British birders through the Texas Hill Country when one of them became deathly ill in the middle of the night. I rushed him and three of his friends to the emergency room at Uvalde Memorial Hospital, twenty-two miles away. After getting out of the car, we heard, then saw, a pair of Eastern Screech-Owls flying around the parking-lot lights. The English birders had never seen the species before.

On a trip to Minnesota one summer, we chalked up numerous parking-lot birds. Driving across the Canadian border north of Roseau, we found a pair of Evening Grosbeaks in the border crossing parking lot. At our motel in Warroad, a Northern Flicker and a flock of Ring-billed Gulls greeted us as we drove in the driveway to check in. At Warroad School Forest an Indigo Bunting serenaded us from a tree at the parking lot's edge. At Tamarac National Wildlife Refuge (NWR) a Red-eyed Vireo, usually a bird of the high canopy, bid us farewell from low in a small tree in front of our car just as we were leaving. It was a Killdeer at our motel in Thief River Falls and an American Bittern in the headquarters pool at Agassiz NWR.

A Common Pauraque sounded off in the McAllen, Texas, Hilton's parking lot after we spent hours searching unsuccessfully for that elusive night bird in the Bentsen–Rio Grande Valley State Park that same evening. It was the Montezuma Quail at McDonald Observatory in the Davis Mountains.

As you casually park your car on any parking lot, be alert. There's no telling what you might see. Why, you might even catch sight of a Gray Hawk, just as we did one spring, soaring above us in front of headquarters at Santa Ana NWR in the Rio Grande Valley, or a Wood Stork at Mrazek Pond in Everglades National Park, or a Green Jay as you pull in to park at Laguna Atascosa NWR headquarters in south Texas, and on and on and on. Why, you can add birds infinitum. ❧

A Paradise for Hummers
and Hummer-lovers

Hundreds of hummers hover and buzz around six feeders hanging from the eaves of the observation building. A variety of songbirds and woodpeckers forage at feeding stations beyond the sugar-water feeders. Scores of butterflies nurse at Mexican sunflower blossoms in the butterfly garden. Wild Turkeys amble by, grazing on acorns and pecans, never once looking up at thirty or forty pairs of eyes ogling them. Each evening, sixty white-tailed deer come to feed.

This is not a national or state wildlife refuge. It is a private ranch 1.8 miles south of Christoval, Texas, near San Angelo. Dan Brown and his brother, Win, inherited the three-thousand-plus acres years ago. The public calls it "Dan Brown's Hummer Haven." Dan and his wife Joann call it "home." In recent years, when other ranchers were starving, Dan decided to diversify to keep the family place intact.

The Browns started with one feeder and a handful of hummingbirds almost forty years ago. When they noticed the hummers fighting over the sugar water, they added another feeder and had more birds. The feisty little birds still fought, so Dan added another feeder, then another. Still more birds. Dan laughingly told the birds they would either have to "get along or starve to death." They evidently learned tolerance. On a typical summer day, Dan mixes three gallons of nectar for the estimated three thousand hummers that visit twenty-two two-liter feeders on his ranch. By the time the hummers are all gone in late September, the Browns will have used more than seven hundred pounds of pure cane sugar.

Harold and I were the first customers to arrive one Saturday morning several years ago. Dan was washing feeders with a garden hose. He explained that he fills them only a quarter full because the solution sours in about four days in the West Texas heat. Then he empties the feeders, cleans them, and replenishes them with fresh liquid.

The birds that hatch at Brown Ranch return the following year. That is why there are so many birds. The population of hummers is so dense that Texas Parks and Wildlife officials have recognized the Browns as the top hummingbird feeders in the state every year since 1995. In the early 1990s, when word spread about this phenomenon in West Texas, birders from all over the country came to see the hummingbirds gather. The Browns soon realized they could generate income and not endanger the birds. They built a cozy guest cottage called "Hummer House" in 1996. It is a charming two-bedroom, two-bath rock house with a living room and a fully stocked kitchen.

To accommodate the hundreds of visitors who keep dropping by to see the hummers, the Browns built a wheelchair-accessible, freestanding observation room between their home and the guesthouse. Reservations are necessary. The thirty-by-sixty-foot building has air conditioning, enough folding chairs for sixty-five people, a restroom, soft drinks, and huge plate-glass windows for optimum viewing. Dan chuckles and says, "We now use wildlife as a cash crop." The place has become as popular as Ramsey Canyon Reserve in southeastern Arizona.

After delivering an informative hour-long narrative, Dan takes visitors into the woods in front of his house. He points out several hummingbird nests within about twenty yards. No one has been able to make an exact count of the number of Black-chinned Hummingbirds that nest on his property. Dan puts out huge balls of raw cotton for the little birds to use as nest lining.

Dan's ranch is a mecca not only for hummingbirds but also for bird banders. From 1995 through August, 2002, 3,511 Black-chinned, 380 Ruby-throated, 11 Rufous, 7 Calliope, 1 Allen's, and 1 Broad-tailed Hummingbird, along with 106 other species of birds, were banded at this oasis in the desert. What draws so many birds to this out-of-the-way place? Its natural setting of live oak and pecan timber and the nearby Concho River. Why so many nesting hummers? Baby hummers need protein as well as nectar to survive. Insects thrive in the live oak and pecan trees that cover the ranch.

Dan is a lapidary expert as well as a hummingbird expert. The sign on the front gate says "BROWN RANCH. TEXAS GEMS. HUMMER HOUSE." After visiting them, there is no doubt in my mind that Dan and Joann Brown are the hummingbird king and queen of Texas. The flying gems of summer are their crown jewels.

I was privileged to be at the ranch on another summer day when Bob and Martha Sargent from Clay, Alabama, were banding hummers. "The purple on the throat about knocks my eyes out every time I see it," Bob quips, a male Black-chinned Hummingbird cupped gently in his large hands. I marvel at how he handles such tiny creatures without harming them. With a special tool he picks up an infinitesimal aluminum band, bends it to the proper size, and places it on the thin leg of a black-chinned hummer like a bracelet. As Bob bands the little dynamos, his soft chatter betrays his feelings for the creatures he describes as "too small to be birds."

"This one is so little, it must be just out of the nest," he banters. "This one has an egg in the vent. I think she'll lay it sometime tonight." "This fellow is hormonally charged. He can't wait to find a female!" After Martha records all the data, Bob tenderly kisses the bird, blesses it, and sends it on its way. I get the idea that the Sargents look at hummers as mystical beings whose secrets we may never learn.

"The more we know about hummers," Martha says, "the more we realize there is to know." The Sargents have banded and studied hummingbirds more than fifteen years. In 1993 they founded The Hummer/Bird Study Group, Incorporated, a nonprofit organization dedicated to the study and preservation of hummingbirds and other neotropical migrants. Mostly, they band ruby-throats on their home turf in Alabama. But they will go anywhere in the East when they hear of a vagrant hummer, especially in a nonbirder's yard. They set up a trap and catch the bird, making a point to let the owners hold the hummer in their hands before releasing it. Bob claims this habit almost always ensures an invitation to come back the next year.

In addition to the eight thousand rubies banded in Clay, the Sargents have banded a dozen other species in the East, where generally it is thought only the ruby-throat exists: black-chinned, rufous, Allen's, broad-tailed, Anna's, buff-bellied, green-breasted mango and broad-billed. The three most exciting were a Calliope in South Carolina, and a Green Violet-ear and Magnificent Hummingbird on Saint Catherine Island, Georgia. The magnificent was the first of its species ever recorded east of the Mississippi. "The most stunning was a white-eared banded by one of our sub-permittees in Gulfport, Mississippi. These kinds of findings vindicate what we've been doing all these years," Bob declares.

Dan Brown invited me to a major bird-banding day one summer when the Sargents were in Texas. Arriving a little before 8 A.M., I found two teams banding hummingbirds and songbirds of many species: Painted Bunting, Summer Tanager, Northern Cardinal, Lesser Goldfinch, Tufted Titmouse, Inca Dove, Ash-throated Flycatcher, and Green Kingfisher to name a few. Ross Dawkins, a chemistry professor at Angelo State University in San Angelo, led the other banding team. A regular at the Brown ranch, Dawkins bands birds there several times a year. This was the Sargents' second summer to be there.

At 4 P.M., someone handed Bob a surprise. A female Broad-tailed Hummingbird, usually considered "a hummer of the Rockies," was the first of its kind banded at Brown's ranch. After we photographed this splendid creature from all angles, Bob placed the bird in my hands. I felt its motor revving against my palm. Then, realizing it was free to go after a few seconds, the bird lifted into the air like a helicopter and disappeared into the tall oaks.

Watching Bob banding and releasing the tiny jewels, I decided banding a hummingbird is like putting a genie in a bottle and tossing it into the ocean. There is no telling where, when, or if it will ever be seen again ᕲ.

Shutter-bird Battle with the Sun

Barbara Garland of Waco is the photographer who shot the beautiful images for my book *The Cardinal*. She has had numerous photos of birds published in birding magazines and other publications. While we were working on *The Cardinal*, she and I went on a birding and photography vacation to Rockport/Fulton, Texas. Around 4:30 P.M. on our last day, we were in the Cape Valero subdivision, an area of wetlands and numerous birds, when we decided to finish the trip with a flourish. We invented a new game and called it "The Great Shutter-bird Battle with the Sun." The object was to see how many species of birds Barbara could photograph before sunset, using the car as a blind.

Our battle between the shutter and the sun started at 4:45 P.M. We immediately went into battle mode. We were like a SWAT team. "Chase and shoot" became our battle cry. Instead of an armored tank and cannon, our tools of war were a Chrysler New Yorker and a camera—ironically, a Canon AE-1 with a 500-mm lens. Sure, it looked like a real gun protruding from the side of a tank, but our "bullets" were film and thus harmless to our "enemies" the birds.

While Barbara concentrated on aiming and shooting, I drove. Inching our way along, eyes darting from side to side like scouts on patrol, we searched for a bird, any bird. Suddenly, Barbara shouted, "There's a Tricolored Heron in breeding plumage. Pull over here." While the bird fed in what seemed a frenzied fury, Barbara shot a full clip of ammo—a whole roll of film—before pausing. While she shot, I sat at the wheel, trying not to breathe so I wouldn't cause unnecessary vibrations in the car. When I thought I couldn't hold my breath another second, Barbara leaned back and invited me to take a look through the lens. I saw practically every feather on the bird's body.

Barbara hastily reloaded the Canon, and we moved on, trying to locate another victim. It turned out to be a Reddish Egret, going into its wild and crazy feeding ritual. I don't know how many shots Barbara took of this fascinating fisherman. I drove slowly down the road; the next bird was a Wilson's Plover. This cousin of the Killdeer has a heavy black bill, one black neck band, and grayish-pink legs. The one we saw was almost too easy to capture on film. Cruising the curvy roads of the subdivision, we wandered away from the wetlands. We found Common Nighthawks napping on the pavement in a cul-de-sac where there were no houses. Their camouflage was so cryptic that we almost missed them. Then Barbara spotted a nighthawk sleeping on a tree limb. The background behind this one was much more photogenic than the ones on the road. Still in the car, we employed our secret weapon of stealth and sneaked up on the sleeping nightjar. Barbara fired away. The bird never even blinked an eye. He never knew he was a "casualty" in our battle with the sun.

As we turned to leave Cape Valero, we spotted a Greater Roadrunner sunbathing in the late afternoon's slanting rays. Fluffing all the feathers on his back, he hunched over to catch a few of those rays before turning in for the night. After straightening all his feathers, he turned and disappeared into the thick brush. Barbara captured him during his sunbath.

Next we drove toward the community of Bayside, where there are extensive marshy areas on both sides of the road. We thought it would be a good place to find more captives. Our first victim was a Black-necked Stilt, a long-legged wading bird that always reminds me of a clown in a tuxedo. He stalked through the water on his ridiculous tall pink stilts. At the water's edge, almost too close to the car to get in the Canon's crosshairs, a Laughing Gull wrestled with a crab, beat it to death on a wooden piling, and swallowed the whole thing in one gulp. A Forster's Tern observed the entire process from his perch on a post in the water, making an easy target for Barbara.

Before crossing the bridge on the west side of Copano Bay, we saw a large puddle of rainwater on a parking lot from which a male Great-tailed Grackle was drinking. Another hostage for our growing list. A Killdeer was bathing in the puddle, too. After finishing his bath he hopped up on a pile of rocks to preen and pose while Barbara shot his picture.

By then it was 6:30 and our time was running out. We returned to a spot we had visited earlier in the day. Along the way, I was forced to bring the car to a screeching halt. Five gorgeous Roseate Spoonbills were coming in for a landing, zeroing in on a pond not far from the car. After that bonanza we headed for Shell Ridge Road. There we found another easy target: a Willet resting atop a fencepost beside the road. While Barbara worked with the Willet, I scanned ahead with my binos to see what might come next. A Black Skimmer was flying low over Aransas Bay, his long lower mandible seeking to strike something edible under the water's surface. Suddenly, his bill snapped shut. He had caught his supper.

Nearer the car, a Ruddy Turnstone seemed mildly curious about our activities. Nevertheless, it went right on with the business of turning over every stone and shell in sight, looking for food underneath. Next to the turnstone was a Sanderling with a band on its leg. Too bad we couldn't read the numbers on the tiny aluminum bracelet. It would have been fun to call the Laurel, Maryland, Bird Banding Lab to find out where the sandpiper had been. A Snowy Egret, standing near the shoreline, pulled his lacy white cloak about his head and strolled out into the water, showing us his golden slippers with each high step he took.

The sun was sinking lower and lower toward the horizon. We decided to move out. When we passed the turnoff to Rockport/Fulton Beach Park, Barbara captured a Great Blue Heron swallowing a large fish.

For our finale, we drove our "tank" across the causeway leading to the old Sea Gun Sportsman's Inn. The only bird in sight was the flying duck on the inn's sign, but that would not do for our game. Just as we were about to give up the battle, we spotted the *pièce de résistance:* a Magnificent Frigatebird soaring high above. I ordered Barbara to get out of the car for this one. The mighty bird was tracing lazy circles in the sky without the slightest flap of its ninety-inch wings. It was then that we noticed there was a full moon rising. I saw the glint in Barbara's eye and knew what she was thinking. "If only I could get a shot of the frigatebird

Frigatebird and the moon, by Sam.

sailing past the face of the moon!" she shouted, her voice trailing off into the sunset.

Playing the role of eternal optimist, I told her to keep her eyes and the Canon focused on the bird while I watched the moon and let her know when the bird was anywhere near the silver sphere. Slowly, slowly, the magnificent bird circled around and around, higher and higher. Barbara followed its every move, panning with the camera, and we feared it would drift too far away. But wait, the "Man o' War" was not about to let us concede the battle. He soon found another thermal between the moon and us. The battle was not over yet. Frantically, I commanded Barbara: "On your mark. Get set. Fire!"

The camera's automatic winder whirred madly. "I think I got it!" Barbara shouted triumphantly. We jumped up and down, celebrating our victory. Our battle between the shutter and the sun was finished. We had won. The striking image of a Magnificent Frigatebird sailing across the face of the moon was our trophy. I think even the man in the moon was smiling.

Wondering aloud, Barbara asked, "How many times in your lifetime do you think you'll see that?" We both already knew the answer. As we drove back across the causeway, Copano Bay swallowed the sun. It was 7:45 P.M.; exactly three hours after our war game began. We thought it ironic that our last casualty was a Man o' War. Quickly tallying the number of victims, we discovered Barbara had captured nineteen species, an average of one species every 9.47 minutes. Not too shabby for the only contestants in this world-class, first-and-last annual Great Shutter-bird Battle with the Sun. ᔒᕈ.

In Love

with a River

In Love with a River

Content in my cabin high above the river
where the loudest sounds are the turning of a page,
the lighting of a candle, the lifting of binoculars to eyes,
the scratch of pen on paper, the soft hoot of an owl,
the spatter of rain on the tin roof,
or the liquid voice of the river,
for a few days I live in a cocoon of anonymity,
with no phone, no TV, no computer,
no voice announcing "You've got mail!"
no set agenda for the day,
no foreign birders knocking at my door
inquiring about vireos, warblers, and buntings.

At the first feathery light of dawn I wake,
not wanting to miss a thing in this holy place.
With the first chink of sunrise a cardinal appears.
It's always the first bird to arrive, the last to depart.
I leave windows open wide to let in feathered song,
wet sounds of rain and river mingled as one voice,
the pungent fragrance of purple sage damp with rain,
and the panoramic view of hills folding back and back
    and back,
as far as I can see,
where the distant thunder echoes from hilltop to valley
    to hilltop,
and back again.

All day long I watch the birds that come to my deck for the
    banquet laid out for them.

I spread peanut butter on a limb for the Carolina Wren.
She laps at it with her tongue like a child licking a Popsicle.
A titmouse grabs a seed then bounces over the wall as if on
    springs.
A chickadee flies roller-coaster fashion to the feeder on the
    Mountain Laurel.
Scrub Jays take turns gobbling half a dozen peanuts, one
    after another,
like collecting beads for a necklace.

While the birds feed on the deck, Monarch butterflies drift
    lazily,
here, then there, high in the sky above the river canyon, even
    in the rain,
and I wonder—How do butterflies survive the pelting rain?
Where do they sleep at night?
How high can they fly?
How much does a Monarch weigh?
So many questions!

The rattle of a kingfisher interrupts my wondering.
I am easily distracted.
I go to the river to watch the kingfisher hunt for his dinner.
He spots a fish in the rushing water, hovers high above it,
dives, and rises from the silver splash, gleaming fish in his
    beak.
I wander across the river bridge to visit once again the
    magical Narnian kingdom
where vireos and warblers danced and played among
    juniper boughs in the spring.
This fall day, onstage, all is silent, like a ghost theater
from which all the thespians have vanished into thin air.

I move on down the road, back toward the river.
Taking the place of spring troubadours in my mind,
fall butterflies suckle at luscious white blossoms.

Cypress roots going down into the river, by Sam.

I look into the sky, and there to my wondering eyes appear
hundreds of Monarchs settling into their leafy, lichen
   bedrooms
in the oaks and mesquites.
They hang in clusters like grapes on a vine,
until the branches are heavy with orange and black gossamer
   wings
folded against the approaching dark.

So this is where they sleep!

Jockeying for space—just one more twig to hang onto—
a lone Monarch flits from cluster to cluster.
Finding no room in the inn, it finally flutters to another tree.

Are the butterflies and birds drawn to this river like I am?

Is it possible to fall in love with a river?
I think so, for when I am away from my river for too long,
I feel a deep longing to be near it,
to hear the voice of its liquid rush,
to feel the embrace of its sensuous rippling folds,
to be engulfed in the arms of its cypress sentinels,
to hear the soft whisper of its tranquil pools.

The single prevalent feature of the river is flux and change.
Through millennia it has chiseled new paths and deposited
    tons of
white river rocks on its shores.
Normally, the river flows like a long, seamless, green silk
    scarf,
sometimes billowing as if lifted on hummingbird wings,
rising and falling gracefully as it cascades over boulders
    worn smooth
by centuries of rushing water washing up its silver spray.

The river is different every time I go there.
I've seen it transformed overnight from a trickling stream
to a raging torrent, its sides swelled beyond belief,
placid bottle-green turned to churning chocolate-brown.

I've stood at water's edge, stooped, and collected stones
    from the river
to place in a Mason jar, filling the jar with the startlingly
    clear liquid.
I want to take a portion of the river home so I can see it
    and dip my fingertips in it
whenever I feel that unbearable longing to be near it.
Were I to take a sip of its cold, refreshing water, it would
    taste better than the best of wines.
It would taste of rock and root and earth and rain—
    water-tumbled rocks,

roots of ancient cypress trees like gnarled knees and arthritic
    fingers
reaching from its limestone banks for sustenance,
and gentle veils, yet sometimes heavy curtains of rain.

A little before dusk, I go to my favorite spot on Earth:
the highest point overlooking Frio Canyon.
Through branches of cypress trees, I look down and see
the shining river winding its way through the canyon
like a coach-whip snake on a dusty country road.
Standing at the edge of the cliff, I wait for great light to give
    way to little light.
The sinking sun's golden glow caresses the hillsides and
    canyon walls,
the cypress canopy, and the river, kissing them goodnight.

Night comes quickly to the Texas Hill Country.
Shining out of the darkness of space, a crescent moon, with a
    star beside it,
softly touches the river, infusing it with silvery light.
For solace, I go to my river sanctuary—where, I am certain,
bright angel feet have trod—and renew my soul and spirit.
I watch the verdant water flow before me and beyond me,
drop by drop, cupful by cupful,
like reviewing the events of my life, knowing full well I can
    never call back
a single drop nor one event.
I try to memorize every detail: the water, the rocks, the sky,
    the birds,
the stars, the trees, the way I feel when I am there, enlivened,
    all my senses keen.
I claim the watercolor landscape, washed in hues of holy
    calm and cathedral quiet,
knowing that in the days to come, the remembrance of this
    "rivertime"

will be the deep well from which my spirit can drink its
sweet amen of peace.

I am in love with a river. ❧

Written in Concan from Cabin 42,
November 1, 2, 3, 4, and 5, 2000
(and I will probably keep revising it ad infinitum)

Best Little Hotspot in Texas

"Did you come to see the little bird?" One of several young women in Cabin 15 at Neal's Lodges directed the question to me. Apparently the women had been plagued by the steady stream of birders who were instructed to "look for the bird behind Cabin 15." Being nonbirders, little did they know or care that the little bird in question was one of the rarest of Texas's birds, the Black-capped Vireo, and only one of many reasons I consider Concan to be the best little hotspot in Texas.

Not only do Black-capped Vireos, Golden-cheeked Warblers, and many other birds find the grounds at Neal's to be hospitable, humans flock there as well. The best time to see the special birds of the area is from mid-March to mid-May, when the lodge is not too crowded. In fact, most of the people visiting Neal's in the spring are birders. However, beginning with Memorial Day weekend the numbers change; Neal's is wall-to-wall "tourists" with not many birders. Neal's has been a popular family vacation spot since the late 1920s, when Tom Neal built the original cabins on the cliffs overlooking the Frio River. Some of Tom's rustic cabins are still in use today, along with numerous new cabins that have been added through the years for a total of over sixty. Camping areas and a few RV hookup sites are also available.

Each cabin is secluded from the others by broad sheltering oaks and ashe junipers (commonly called "cedars"), ideal habitat for Black-capped Vireos and Golden-cheeked Warblers. Some cabins have a great view of the pristine Frio River as it flows through the Frio Canyon. Towering over the river are jagged vertical cliffs where Great Horned Owls may nest in its caves or roost in the sun, and Mexican Free-tailed Bats sometimes emerge at dusk; and always, the liquid notes of Canyon Wrens cascade down those hallowed walls at all hours of the day. The banks of the Frio are lined with centenarian bald cypress trees with roots reaching far out into the cold, blue-green water. It is an ideal place to look for Green Kingfishers, Cave Swallows, and Black Phoebes, or simply "tubing" down the Frio on a hot afternoon.

With the exception of a brief period in 1983, this vacation spot has been owned and operated by some member of the Neal family, beginning with Tom's daughter, Mary Tom Buchanan, and her husband, John, who took over after Tom gave it up. Tom's granddaughter, Mary Anna Roosa, and her husband Rodger now manage the place. They own it jointly with Tom's grandson, John S. Graves, Jr., and his wife Carol. Mary Anna runs the lodge from the country store, where twin oaks shade the entrance and Blue Bell Ice Cream (a Texas specialty) awaits the hot and hungry birder. Rodger manages the café. There you may enjoy Texas-style cooking that will satisfy even the biggest appetite. Neal's Café has the best chicken-fried steak I have ever eaten, barbecued chicken or brisket, fish, vegetables, salads, and melt-in-your-mouth hot rolls swimming in butter and locally harvested honey.

The owners realize the importance of maintaining the habitat for the birds. Consequently, they have done nothing to alter conditions that are just right for two species that have been on the endangered species list for more than fifteen years, the star avian attractions of the Texas Hill Country: Black-capped Vireo and Golden-cheeked Warbler. These two birds alone offer incentive enough for the birder who keeps a Life List to come to this idyllic place that time seems to have forgotten. Birders from all parts of the world come to Concan just to see these two birds. In the process they get a bonus, because many other birds that were formerly considered "Rio Grande Valley Birds" can be seen on the grounds at Neal's. For example, Long-billed Thrasher, Olive Sparrow, Hooded Oriole, Black-bellied Whistling-Duck, and White-winged and Inca Doves are all seen there regularly. On rare occasions, lucky birders may spot a Ringed Kingfisher flying up and down the Frio, or a Great Kiskadee calling from the top of a cypress.

Even though never considered very common, as recently as fifty years ago the Black-capped Vireo (*Vireo atricapillus*) was somewhat common throughout much of Central Texas. My friend, Wally Christian, a lifelong Texas birder, remembers the blackcap's song from his boyhood days around Dallas. Since its discovery in 1851, much has been learned about the distribution and habits of the Black-capped Vireo. We now know that it winters in western Mexico from southern Sinaloa and Durango, south to Michoacan. It has also been recorded in Tamaulipas, Mexico, during the winter.

At one time, the blackcap's historical breeding range reached from central Coahuila in northern Mexico, northward throughout Kansas, and into the southeastern corner of Nebraska. But no more. Sadly, due to the loss of habitat in recent years, its breeding range has been greatly reduced. Today, only a few pairs remain in Oklahoma, and the Texas and Coahuila populations are declining as well. Blackcaps are scattered over an estimated thirty to fifty enclaves of suitable habitat. Special studies indicate that perhaps fewer than two thousand individuals remain in existence. Not only has loss of habitat contributed greatly to the blackcap's decline, but the Brown-headed Cowbird also has heavily parasitized the species.

The Black-capped Vireo is a diminutive bird about the size of a Ruby-crowned Kinglet. When searching for it, set aside any preconceived ideas you may have of vireos, such as, "plain of plumage, lethargic of movement, and the females lay speckled eggs." The blackcap violates all vireo norms. It is strikingly handsome and bold of pattern, quick acting, and the female lays pure white eggs.

Almost from the time the blackcap was discovered, it was thought that the sexes were alike, as is the case with most vireos. However, the two are slightly different in plumage. The male blackcap is the only North American vireo with a jet-black head combined with pure white spectacles broken by a spot of black above the eye. His back, shoulders, and rump are light green-gray. His underparts are white, and he has yellowish flanks and two yellow wing bars on each wing. The female is slate gray where the male is black, and her wing bars are white. The olive-green on her back is duller than the male's. Both the male and female have piercing red eyes set off by their keyhole-shaped spectacles.

The blackcap is reclusive as well as being overly active and quick of flight, making it extremely difficult to view. One more easily sees the fluttering branch where the bird *was* an instant before, than where the bird *is*. With a bird that has reclusive habits, it pays to know its song, making the ear a better instrument than the eye for trying to locate it. Since the blackcap is on the endangered species list, both federally and in Texas, it is against the law to harass it in any way. This includes using tape recordings of its song to draw it into view. You must familiarize yourself with its vocalizations if you expect to find it. Even then, unfortunately, the bird usually sings its disjointed, chattering song while perched on an interior, hidden twig of a bush. However, once you hear its distinctive sounds, if you exercise a little patience, sooner or later the bird is almost sure to pop to the top of a bush and give you a chance for a view.

Midday heat usually depresses the songs of most bird species, but it seems to have the opposite effect on the blackcap. Once I spent an entire morning looking for the vireo, beginning behind Cabin 15. Although I heard its harsh, squeaky song repeatedly, I gave up any hope of seeing it. Then, about noon, I heard its disjointed song coming from somewhere near the road at the top of the hill behind Neal's Store. I looked up just in time to see a blackcap fly to a juniper tree and garner a strand of spider's silk with his bill. He took the precious stuff, flew a few yards down the hill, and disappeared inside a bush. I imagine its cozy nest was in that bush.

A blackcap nest is normally even more difficult to locate than the bird itself. The deep, cuplike nest, like its builder, is usually hidden within a bush or small tree that has dense foliage. It is suspended in the fork of two slender twigs from two to six feet above the ground. The nest is made of bark strips, dried leaves, grasses, and other plant fibers. I have seen three active blackcap nests. All of them followed this pattern, and all three were on the grounds at Neal's.

Another rare bird at Neal's is the Golden-cheeked Warbler (*Dendroica chrysoparia*). It should be a little easier to see than the vireo since it usually sings from an exposed perch at the top of a tree. Here again, it pays to know its song, because you almost always hear it before you see it. You must listen carefully for its soft "bzzzz layzee dayzee" that ends on a high note or you will miss it. The bird is almost always closer to you than the song would indicate.

The male goldencheek is similar to the male Black-throated Green Warbler. The two are easily mistaken for one another. The male goldencheek has a distinctive dark line through the eye and lacks the clearly outlined ear patch of the black-throated green. The goldencheek has no yellow on its underparts and is black above, with a black crown, black bib, and black streaks on the sides. Female and immature male goldencheeks are duller than the adult male, and their upper parts are olive with dark streaks; the chin, yellowish or white; and the sides of the throat, streaked. The immature female has less black underneath.

The goldencheek nests nowhere else in the world but on the Edwards Plateau and in similar habitats in Central Texas. A true "native Texan," it is the only bird on the North American list that nests only in Texas. From its winter home in southern Mexico and Guatemala, the Golden-cheeked Warbler arrives in Texas in early to mid-March and begins singing to claim its territory as soon as it arrives. That is why it's important to be in Concan between March and early May. The bird becomes more and more elusive and silent as nesting activities accelerate.

So strong is its preference for the bark of mature ashe junipers for nesting material, it inhabits only those counties in Texas that contain mature junipers. Dense stands of these junipers are locally called "cedar brakes." The warblers don't necessarily nest in the junipers, but they must have the long strips of bark from these trees to weave into their basket-shaped nests. No other material will do.

Once I was leading a group on a bird walk in Lost Maples State Natural Area near Concan. We were surprised and delighted when we saw a pair of Golden-cheeked Warblers working on their nest in a big-tooth maple near the hiking trail. A mature ashe juniper was nearby and the birds made repeated trips to the trunk of that tree to extract loose strips of bark. The warbler is a master of camouflage. Ideal nesting habitat for the goldencheek is found in juniper-oak woodlands distributed along steep scarps and canyons and may contain various proportions of oaks: plateau live oak, Texas oak, Lacey oak, Shumard oak, and shin oak. Other trees may be Texas ash, redbud, escarpment chokecherry, bumelia, cedar elm, pecan, Arizona walnut, and in some areas, the rare Texas madrone. A diversity of grasses, shrubs, vines, and wildflowers is also important. Since goldencheeks are insectivorous, it follows that the more diverse the habitat, the greater the variety of insects. It helps if water is nearby.

In the excitement of your quest for these two special birds, don't blink while driving toward Concan or you might miss it. It is at the intersection of U.S. Highway 83 and State Highway 127, eighty miles west of San Antonio (via U.S. Highway 90), and twenty-three miles north of Uvalde (via U.S. Highway 83). Many birders fly into San Antonio, rent a car, and drive to Concan.

Remember to take your eyes off the birds once in a while. The Frio River below Neal's Lodges has been touted by *Southern Living* magazine as one of the most scenic swimming holes on the cypress-lined river. *Texas Monthly* says it is "one of the most spectacular spots in the state . . . a small marvel that time has overlooked." The National Audubon Society describes Concan as one of the best bird-watching areas in the United States. With a combination of splendid birds, larrapin' food, and breath-taking scenery, what more incentive do you need to visit the best little hotspot in Texas? What are you waiting for? Be sure to tell them June sent you. ᶭ

Bathing Beauties of the Frio River

From my folding chair by the bridge I could see several small pools of water among the rocks at the edge of the Frio River. I felt like a "peeping Tom" as I watched a female Painted Bunting busy at her toilette. Looking all around to make sure no danger was imminent, she dipped first her chest and then her head into the cold water. She flipped droplets of the refreshing liquid over her greenish back, shook all over, then flew to a branch at water's edge and began preening.

A spot on the river a hundred yards downstream from "the best little swimming hole in Texas" is a place I now claim as "the best little bird-bathing hole in Texas." I discovered it one year after the last of my Elderhostel groups left Concan, and I had a few days of R and R just for myself. One evening after dinner, I wandered down to the river with my folding chair and settled in for whatever would happen. The late afternoon sun filled the hills and cliffs with golden light and reflected silhouettes of the stately cypress trees in the green water. If I were an artist I would paint a picture of this scene and hang it in my home to remind me of the mystique of the place, which draws me back time and time again.

I soon discovered it was a favorite place for birds to bathe. Within just a few minutes I wracked up a baker's dozen species coming to drink and bathe. For years since, I have watched the feathered bathing beauties of the Frio River every chance I get. The spot is at the edge of the shallow river, where pools form among the stones and create ideal places for small birds to congregate at bath time. It almost seems to be a social activity for the birds. The splashing of one bird attracts another, then another, and another. I discovered show time was almost any time of day that I happened to be there.

Another April, after my final group had left, I again took my chair and made the short jaunt down to the river. Neal's is on busy Texas State Highway 127, which joins U.S. Highways 83 and 90 from Concan to Sabinal. Caution signs and flashing yellow lights on both sides of Neal's warn motorists they are in a "recreational area." Unfortunately, few drivers heed the warnings and speed on through. However, on that particular morning, more than a few drivers slowed down to see what I was looking at. Curiosity got the better of one driver, who stopped and got out of his pickup around noon. He said he had been driving since 7 A.M. and needed a rest. Seeing me gave him a good excuse to stop since he's a birder, too. When he saw the variety of birds coming to bathe, he went back to his truck to get his binoculars. Sitting on the rounded river stones beside me for ten minutes, he added three new birds to his Life List before going on his way refreshed.

Appropriately enough, the first birds I saw that day were male and female Painted Buntings, my favorite bird. Added to this rainbow of colors, Lesser Goldfinches were the most abundant birds to use these bathing facilities. About half the size of House Sparrows, the males are coal black on the back and lemon yellow on the front. The females are olive green on the back and duller yellow on the front, similar to female American Goldfinches. However, the lesser has dark legs and the American pink ones. So, when in doubt about the identity of the females of these two species, check out the color of their legs.

In my view at one time were a male Blue Grosbeak, male and female Northern Cardinals, Lesser Goldfinches, male and female Summer Tanagers, and bright red male House Finches. A Western Scrub-Jay hopped out of the bushes and onto a rock in the middle of one of the pools. His blue reflection in the placid water looked as if he were standing on a mirror. A Lazuli Bunting at the edge of the gravel bar took me by surprise. I don't often see this species in the area. He darted to the pool and infused it with a split second of turquoise jewels before disappearing into the brush. What an extravagant array of colors!

A Long-billed Thrasher waded into the water and bathed. Then it flew across the river to preen. Two tiny Bushtits splashed into the shallowest edge. I would have missed them had it not been for a male Indigo Bunting catching my attention with his deep violet-blue plumage. All the time I was watching this kaleidoscope of colors, Barn Swallows swooped low for insects and sips of water, leaving long liquid Vs in their wake. Their nests were in the rafters on the front porches of the cabins overlooking the river. Northern Rough-winged Swallows hawked insects above the water's surface, delivering them to nestlings tucked into crevices in the huge boulders in the middle of the Frio.

A Green Kingfisher flew low over the water, swooping upward to a perch on a log that was stuck in the shallow river. A Spotted Sandpiper teetered its way along a gravel bar searching for tidbits to eat. Walking like a seesaw, its head and tail bobbed alternately with every step. A Solitary Sandpiper followed the seesawing bird. As if in training for the Olympics, a pair of Black Phoebes flew swiftly and low from the highway bridge to a gravel bar at midriver on forays for insects. They were feeding young in a nest under the bridge. Four kinds of doves came to drink or bathe: White-winged, Mourning, Inca, and Common Ground-Doves. After watching them, I noted that White-winged Doves have a different way of drinking than smaller birds. Instead of dipping only their bills into the water and then throwing their heads back to allow the liquid to flow down their throats, they dip their entire head into the water as if drinking from a straw. They simply sip and swallow with their heads submerged. I learn something new every time I go out to watch birds.

A variety of sparrows showed up: Lark Sparrows with beautiful facial markings, making them easy to identify; Clay-colored, White-crowned, and Lincoln's Sparrows passing through on their northward migratory journeys; Olive Sparrows that nest at Neal's; resident Chipping Sparrows that sport bright rufous caps, a dark line through the eye, white eyebrows, and white wing bars; and Rufous-crowned Sparrows with somewhat duller rufous caps.

While enjoying the sights in silent awe, I suddenly heard a familiar soft hum and turned my head just in time to see a female Black-chinned Hummingbird hovering briefly above the water. After turning her body in all directions she dipped only her tail in the water. Rising a few inches, she hovered and then dipped again, her tail and belly both touching the water this time. Finally, she found a place shallow enough to stand for a more thorough soaking.

Since 1995, I have seen a total of sixty-four species drinking and bathing at these enticing pools. What a way to watch birds! Just sit back and let the birds come to you and the water. I'm glad I was there to catch the performances of so many "Bathing Beauties of the Frio River." 〜

"Rivertime"

It's a gift we give ourselves, this "rivertime" in Concan. Short days are filled with birds and poetry by the pristine Frio, tea ceremonies with blue calico teapots and teacups, meals that are never "just meals," gifts wrapped in pansy paper, picnics at our favorite spot on the river, writing in our journals, making lists of holy moments. Lazy days when we don't get up until we want to, stay in our pajamas until noon, and eat when and what we want. For once in our lives we eat ice cream for breakfast. Long evenings are filled with candlelight and billions of stars. We can actually see the Milky Way from our pallet on the picnic table and remember that Mary Magdalene, Mother Teresa, Betsy Ross, and Helen Keller saw these same stars. (Well, maybe not Helen Keller, but Annie Sullivan told her about them.) If we are lucky, "shooting stars" surprise us while I converse mystically with the Great Horned Owl who-o-o lives across the river.

If "anticipation is half the trip," we have a year to anticipate this wonder of wonders, this annual "friendship retreat" beyond description. Sharlande and I make our lists of things to take: menus for the week, grocery lists, books we intend to read but never do, pots, pans, dishes, purple sheets, cinnamon, quilts, CDs, and CD player. We must not forget Anthony Way singing our anthem for the week, "For the Beauty of the Earth."

We get out the purple trunk and bubble wrap, for, as John Thomas Carlisle wrote, "It is good to use best china, treasured dishes, the most genuine goblets," and the oldest lace doilies, the purple plaid tablecloth, linen napkins, and the wedding silverware. Candles, and more candles, Mawmaw's candle holders, Ebby's crystal goblets, babka, books, and bird-seeds, a vase for wildflowers we pick each day, and the egg poacher for Eggs Benedict with the best hollandaise sauce on the planet.

Between us we pack six cameras. We don't want to miss a thing, from piles of fruits and vegetables to "golden-cheeked" eggs on cobalt blue dishes, baked sweet potatoes swimming in butter, chicken legs, and exclamations of, "We're such good cooks!"

We take pictures of our cabin before we transform it from prebasic drab to post–J & S flashes of brightness, and after, purple T-shirts cover russet-orange kitchen chairs. A long plaid cloth of lavender, aquamarine, and blue hides the orange and brown flower picture on the wall. We decorate the walls with our own photos of pansies and the river and Ecuadorian children. We toss a purple plaid chenille throw over June's chair. Quilts, along with purple sheets and pillows, on the beds blend with the rest of our decor. We build pyramids with the myriad ice chests and boxes of tea, hang colorful tea towels on the refrigerator door and the cabinet drawers, take Polaroid pictures to stick on the fridge, and then take pictures of the pictures.

Even though the sign says "Please Do Not Move the Furniture" we turn the chairs toward the bay window, the better to view birds by day and stars by night. We transform the purple trunk into a tea table, put the floor lamp beside Sharlande's bed so she can read or write in it, turn the recliner toward the kitchen so June can rest while Sharlande chops and cooks, and we won't miss a beat of the conversation that never ends.

When the time comes to pack all our treasures into the Suburban, it is like putting a puzzle together: purple trunk toward the middle of the cargo area; ice chests in front of the trunk; fragile stuff on the third seat so it doesn't get squashed; cameras, binoculars, and scope on the second seat in case we need them on the way; luggage wherever there is room (*if* there is room); folding lawn chairs behind the driver's seat.

"We may need a U-Haul this year!" Sharlande moans. Our lists of "stuff" get longer every year. But so do our memories—memories of "Rivertime in Concan" from which our souls can draw strength and peace for the rest of our days. §➷

American Nightingales of Concan

Sharlande and I tried to squeeze every ounce of pleasure out of the last of our ten days in Concan. Driving to our favorite spots, we took pictures of the swimming hole, the picturesque twisted cypress south of the bridge, the grove of live oaks on the hill overlooking the river, the towering cypress trees in splashes of glorious fall colors reflecting in the Frio River, and my favorite spot in all the world at the top of the cliff. Suddenly, we were out of film.

We drove back to the cabin and Sharlande dashed in to get more film. While waiting in the Suburban, I noticed water dripping from a faucet attached to a tree in front of the cabin next door. A subtle movement drew my attention to the ground four feet below the faucet. A Hermit Thrush, whose russet brown back matched the color of the dead leaves on the ground, dipped its head repeatedly into the water collecting in a depression in the rocky soil. I got out of the Suburban and tiptoed to the picnic table twenty feet away for a better look. Oblivious to my presence, the thrush drank as if it could not get enough.

As you might guess by its name, the Hermit Thrush is normally a shy, solitary bird. I have never seen more than one at a time, so I was totally unprepared for what happened next. A second Hermit Thrush suddenly appeared on the rock wall beyond the faucet. After alighting, the bird raised its rufous tail and then lowered it slowly, a behavior unique to this species of thrush. It joined the first thrush at the refreshing fountain. Like a falling leaf, another thrush drifted down from the tree above. As if that were not enough, a fourth hermit sailed in on silent wings from another direction, then a fifth. I could not believe my eyes, for here was a veritable throng of thrushes. "Shhhh," I mimed to Sharlande when she came out of the cabin, all the while motioning for her to sneak around behind the picnic table to watch the show.

Instead of merely drinking from the font, one thrush plunged in with its whole body and splashed around until it was thoroughly soaked. Another flew to the spigot, bent double, and caught droplets of water dripping from the faucet. With an entire river a hundred feet below, all this bird needed was one drop at a time. A Golden-fronted Woodpecker, playing "follow the leader," announced its presence with a loud cackle, attached itself to the tree, contorted its body backward, and took a drink from the spigot.

Appropriately, thrush rhymes with "hush." Hermit Thrushes generally skulk silently on the forest floor where their brown backs and freckled breasts blend with the leaf litter. It is easy to overlook them unless you hear their distinctive "chuck" call notes. Living up to their name, only in winter do Hermit Thrushes join other species in foraging flocks. Even then they usually remain on the fringes of the flock, staying to themselves. The Hermit Thrush (*Catharus guttatus*) winters over much of the south and southwest. It is found in breeding season at only two locations in Texas, my home state: the higher elevations of the Guadalupe and Davis Mountains. Both ranges have stands of pine, juniper, Douglas fir, and oak at elevations of seven thousand feet and up. This montane, evergreen forest habitat is exactly what the reclusive hermit needs.

So quiet are they in winter that one might never guess the Hermit Thrush is one of the most renowned songsters of the bird world. In the remote forests where it breeds, however, the Hermit Thrush sings its exquisite, flutelike song, charming the few people who are lucky enough to hear it. So rich and clear is its song, rising and falling like the flowing Frio, that someone nicknamed it the "American Nightingale."

Up until that November afternoon in Concan, in all my years of birding I had heard the ethereal, bell-like tones of the Hermit Thrush once: in southeastern Arizona. As I wrote these words, remembering the "American Nightingales" of Concan, I listened to a recording of their song and felt transported to a thickly wooded canyon in Arizona. In my imagination the notes faded away in a silvery tinkle as I again with Walt Whitman exulted, "O liquid and free and tender . . ." 🐦

On the Edge of Our Seats

Seven birders sloshed through the marsh, walking as quietly as possible. We didn't want to disturb the birds foraging on the mudflats in front of the hide. Quiet though we were, the birds sensed our presence and scattered for cover. We filed into the wooden structure and silently took our seats facing the closed windows. Our guide would open them only after the birds settled down to their normal activities.

We sat on the edge of our seats, senses keen, expectations high. Our leader, Bryan Bland, whispered, "This always reminds me of Christmas morning when as a child I waited breathlessly for the signal to open the packages." Six birders had traveled thousands of miles to bird with Bryan, one of England's foremost ornithologists. Now we sat breathlessly, awaiting his signal to open the windows so we could glimpse the wonders in store for us in this magical place, East Anglia. Finally, the waiting was over. The open windows revealed an array of shorebirds most of us had never seen before. Our high expectations were fulfilled.

Every time I open the blinds at my birding window at home or go on a bird excursion, I'm on the edge of my seat, anxiously waiting for whatever the day holds. One fall day Sharlande and I had been reading beside the Frio River all afternoon, when at dusk we heard, "Whoo-whoo—who-who-who—whoooo." At first the sound was so soft and indistinct I thought I had imagined it, but then it came again, louder than before, and I knew *Bubo virginianus* was about to take off for its night of hunting.

The Great Horned Owl's haunting call, wild as howling wolves, interrupted our reverie, so we moved two hundred yards upstream. Looking up, we saw that mighty creature of the dark perched on the edge of night. Calling again, he pumped his powerful, silent wings and stole away into the twilight, like a shadow on slow, measured wing beats.

One evening the previous spring, during one of my Elderhostels, I was scouting out the same area along the Frio. The oblong cave high on the face of the cliff above the river had intrigued me during the many years I had led birding tours and Elderhostels at Neal's. On many occasions I saw a lone Great Horned Owl sunning in the cave opening. On this particular evening, not only was there an adult Great Horned Owl standing on the ledge, but also, like an apparition, the downy form of an owlet crept slowly from behind its mother. She began to nuzzle her downy offspring. It was the first time I had ever seen young in the cave. I was ecstatic.

Racing back to my cabin to get my scope, I saw four Elderhostelers watching birds from the front porch of their cabin. Hurriedly, I told them of my discovery and asked if they would like to join me. When we got to the right spot, I set up the scope and focused on the endearing little family. The owls put on quite a show, creating a scene that would have made a perfect picture for a Mother's Day card. Yet even the most powerful of telescopic lenses could not reach that far across the river or as high as the cave. Although we could not photograph the scene, the image will remain engraved in our memories for a long, long time.

The next day, I took the whole group to see if the owls were still on the ledge. Sure enough, they were. For the next three weeks I took scores of birders to the site as often as possible. On each visit we marveled at the owlet's rate of growth and development. One evening during my last week in Concan, the baby was at one end of the cave opening and its mother was at the other. Several minutes later, the father ambled out of the darkness of the cave to join the other two. By this time the owlet had grown to about two-thirds the height of its parents and lost its natal down. It already had white throat feathers resembling a papal collar, and its wings were fully feathered. The owlet seemed to enjoy hopping around, stretching its wings. Once in a while it came so near the edge of the cliff that everyone gasped, fearing it might topple over the side to certain death from its precipitous perch. Thankfully, it never did.

The facial discs around its eyes had become quite distinct, giving it the appearance of having great wisdom for its young age. In fact, it looked like a professor in full academic regalia, swaying back and forth, "hands" on hips. A mortarboard cap would have made the image complete. Because Great Horned Owls are known to live for more than twenty-eight years, I have probably seen the same pair during each of my trips to Concan, giving me a special connection with this family. One night, hearing the familiar "Whooo-whooo, who-who-who," I echoed "Whooo-whooo, who-who-who." The owl called again, and I quickly sent my response on wings of night. The owl and I "conversed" in this manner for several minutes, back and forth across the dark river.

Great Horned Owls may begin their nesting season as early as January or February. They typically nest in abandoned hawk, eagle, heron, raven, or crow nests, in trees, on cliffs, in caves, and sometimes on the ground. The only nesting materials they add are down feathers from their own breasts. The female lays as many as three almost spherical white eggs. While she does most of the incubating, the male brings her food. The eggs hatch asynchronously in twenty-six to thirty-five days. The pair at Concan had only one owlet that we ever saw. Though outwardly alike, it is easy to tell the female from the male by her larger size, especially when the two are standing side by side.

The young may leave the nest during the sixth to eighth weeks, but the parents still take care of them. At this age they are capable of only short flights. The fledgling stage lasts for another three months, during which time they develop more highly skilled flying and hunting techniques. At about five months of age they are ready to live independently, away from their parents. I regretted that I was unable to stay around long enough to see the young owlet gain its independence. From the edge of my seat in Waco, I could only imagine the drama that unfolded on the edge of the cliff in Concan. ❧

The Owl

BY HAROLD OSBORNE

So silent through the night he glides
In search of him who, knowing, hides,
And with each careful, measured breath
Awaits the wait of coming death.

His beak so sharp, his talons strong,
His soft, soft wings move him along,
Until his eyes with owlish powers
Focus on the one who cowers

Beneath the leaf and waits the hours
For dawn and life—or owl-dealt death.

'Tis Nature's way, we often say,
And so it is; but how to stay
The victim's end and yet leave free
The fit's survival remains the key
To accepting that which has to be.
The lesson learned, like a two-edged knife
Cuts clean both ways—from death comes life.

Have pity then for him who gives
His own life's breath for the one who lives;
But know, for all, that life is short.
Each must serve as death's escort.

Be we owl or mouse, airborne, earthbound,
We live life best when we have found
Our own small niche and fill it well.
Leave Him who judges all to tell
How we have done. ༃

Birds Love Neal's, Too

"Take wing, explore, sing once more.
But realize when ends the quest,
O'er all love cries, "The nest! The nest!"
—Harold Osborne

Matthew 8:20 tells us, "Foxes have holes, and the birds of the air have nests." Every living creature has some sort of home. Snails carry theirs on their backs. Prairie dogs have burrows. Some bats live in caves. Some types of wasps build paper houses. Aphids live on plants. Ants live in the ground. A Green Anole lives in the English ivy twining around my mailbox. The list goes on and on.

It seems that birds find the grounds at Neal's Lodges to be equally as appealing as the participants in my birding groups. One spring, when I was leading small groups of birders and conducting three birding Elderhostels back to back at Neal's, we found more nests than I ever remember finding. Over twenty different species were either building or already sitting on nests, ranging from the walnut-sized nest of a hummingbird to the Great Horned Owls' nest on the cliff's ledge. I concluded that the more keen eyes we had scouting the area, the more nests we would find.

One of the most interesting we found was a Bushtit nest. The Bushtit is a tiny gray bird with a long tail and a Latin name almost as long as the bird: *Psaltriparus minimus.* Its genus name comes from a Greek word *psaltris,* meaning a player of the lute or zither, and *parus,* meaning titmouse. Its species name comes from a word meaning least. The Bushtit, measuring three and three-quarters inches to four and a half inches long, is one of the smallest of North American birds.

The Bushtit's nest is absolutely amazing for such a small bird. Usually suspended from a limb in plain sight, it is a gourd-shaped pocket, six to twelve inches or more in length, and so well camouflaged that it looks like a small log hanging in the tree. The nest we found in 1996 was in a large live oak tree; others since then were in juniper and mesquite trees. Bushtit nests can be anywhere from six to thirty-five feet above the ground; the ones at Neal's are about twelve feet up.

A fascinating fact about a Bushtit nest is that it takes the birds thirteen to fifty-one days to construct it, mostly of small twigs, mosses, rootlets, lichens, oak leaves, and flowers bound with spider's silk. Both sexes help, and the finished nest is a work of art. The entry hole is on the side near the top. Inside and below the hole, a horizontal passage leads to the bowl near the bottom where the female lays five to seven white eggs. The birds use plant down, wool, fur, hair, and feathers to line the nest. Male and female take turns incubating the eggs, and both birds sleep in the nest at night. When we found the first nest, the parents were already feeding nestlings. They made numerous trips carrying insects to and from the nest.

Wrens are notorious for nesting in unusual places. Any little nook or cranny will do: in open ends of pipes, clothespin bags, barbecue pits, over-turned quart jars, washtubs, hanging baskets, birdhouses, mailboxes, woodpecker holes, bicycle baskets, on tractors, exhaust pipes of pickup trucks, holes in rock walls, and so forth. There is even a record of Canyon Wrens nesting in the dome of the state capitol in Austin, Texas. The hole through which the birds entered was a broken window. After the window was repaired, "the nation's largest wren house" was put out of business.

As you might guess, the Canyon Wren prefers to live in steep rocky canyons, especially near water. One nest at Neal's was in a highly unusual place. For days the Elderhostelers and I saw a Canyon Wren foraging out-side the door of Neal's laundry room. The bird sang its descending song, gathered insects off the grills of parked cars, and then disappeared into what we thought was a vent pipe at the edge of the laundry room roof. One day, someone doing their laundry saw the wren fly through a hole over the hot-water heater and dart into an opening above some cupboards. When I heard about it, I took the class to the laundry room and we climbed onto a table to view the bird sitting on its well-hidden, open-cup nest. Our curiosity did not seem to bother the wren at all.

Through the years, Elderhostelers and I have found the nests of four species of vireos on the grounds at Neal's: white-eyed, black-capped, yellow-throated, and Bell's. One April day, I was strolling along the Rio Frio with a group, when we heard and then saw a Yellow-throated Vireo repeatedly returning to the same spot on a horizontal limb. When I fo-cused the scope on it, we discovered the beautiful vireo was working on a nest about twenty feet from the ground. Checking on its progress over the next few days, we learned that both sexes constructed the thick-walled nest using grasses and strips of inner bark woven together with spider silk and plant down. The finished nest was a hanging basket attached to a young cypress tree limb with strands of spider webs. Bits of gray lichen decorated the outside of the basket, so it blended perfectly with its surroundings. Each time we passed that way, we saw one of the pair, both of whom incu-bate the eggs, sitting on the nest. When I left Concan several days later, they were still sitting. When I returned for a brief visit two weeks after that, I found an empty nest. Someone reported that a day or two before I returned, the parents were feeding the fledglings outside the nest.

Smaller than the Yellow-throated Vireo's nest, the white-eyed's was attached to the crotch of a tiny limb in a small juniper, less than two feet off the ground. We heard the bird sing from the trees surrounding the nest site, so it did not surprise us when a sharp-eyed Elderhosteler spied the nest as the bird flew into the secluded spot. The concealed nest was at the edge of one of the roads at Neal's where cars and pickups pass by dozens of times each day, but the incubating bird never flinched. The three Black-capped Vireo nests I have seen at Neal's were all about four feet off the ground and well hidden from view. Bell's Vireo nests are usually six to eight feet off the ground and located in small oak or mesquite trees. We found all the vireo nests first by hearing the birds sing. When I returned to Concan two weeks after my Elderhostels were over, all the nests were empty, even the Great Horned Owls'. Apparently, all the nestlings fledged in my absence, and I literally began to feel the effects of "the empty nest syndrome." ❦

Nose to Beak with Hummingbirds

In her book *Bird by Bird,* Anne Lamott says you should write about what you see through a one-inch picture frame. My "one-inch picture frame" during spring break every year is a bay window in my favorite cabin at Neal's. The cliff-top cabin overlooks Frio Canyon and commands a panoramic view of the cypress-lined river and layer upon layer of hills. A hundred and one steps (our grandson Wheeler counted them) lead to the swimming hole directly below.

After settling in, I place a hummingbird feeder, birdseed, and a makeshift birdbath on the deck of the cabin in front of the bay window. I think the birds know to look for me because about five minutes after the "table" is set, they begin showing up. House Finches are almost always first to arrive. Their twittering seems to say: "She's back. Let's go tell everyone." Soon a host of birds show up to investigate.

During our spring visit in 1999, one surprise guest was a female Pyrrhuloxia, *Cardinalis sinuatus,* easily mistaken for its first cousin, the Northern Cardinal. I had seen it in the area before, but never on the deck of our cabin. Its most distinguishing features are a thick, yellow, parrotlike beak and a crest that is taller than the cardinal's. During that week, the Pyrrhuloxia showed up frequently to stock up on its favorite food: black-oil sunflower seeds.

That week our window framed Western Scrub-Jay (the blue jay without a crest), Spotted Towhee (the western form of what was formerly called Rufous-sided Towhee), Long-billed Thrasher, Yellow-throated Vireo, Northern Cardinal, seven species of sparrows (including two of my favorites, olive and clay-colored), and Canyon, Bewick's, and Carolina Wrens. Before the week was out we had seen forty-six bird species without leaving our cabin.

A male Black-chinned Hummingbird arrived on Tuesday. Its black gorget (throat patch) flashed iridescent amethyst when the light caught it just right. It was almost a perfect match for the mountain laurel blossoms still clinging to the bushes on our deck. Male Ruby-throated Hummingbirds and female blackchins arrived a day later.

Cold, wet weather kept Harold and me inside most of the week, but we didn't mind. After all, we were there strictly for R and R. The scene through our "one-inch picture frame" was an ever-changing display of wings and color, so we were never bored. The rest of our family from Waco and Lubbock got there late Friday night. Shortly after their arrival, the window framed a spectacular light show during a raging thunderstorm.

Saturday dawned picture perfect, the rugged hills washed clean by the storm. Since it was too cold to play in the river, our Lubbock grandchildren—fourteen-year-old Wheeler and sixteen-year-old Kelsey—decided to watch birds with their grandmother. They have learned through the years that it pleases me when they say, "Take us birding, Mama June."

As we sat on the picnic table, I showed Kelsey and Wheeler how to adjust the binoculars for their eyes only. I tried to teach them the differences between the Rufous-crowned and Chipping Sparrows that were feeding on the deck. The rufous crown has a black moustache and white eye rings that the chipping lacks. The chipping has white wing bars that the rufous crown doesn't have. The rufous crown is usually solitary; chippings are gregarious. Both have rufous crowns.

Suddenly, a stunning winged visitor swooped past, catching all of us off guard. Its wingtips brushed the mountain laurel eight feet from our faces. At first I thought it was a Turkey Vulture because vultures often cruise by at eye level. However, when I got my binoculars on it and saw barred flight feathers and a banded tail, I realized it was a rare Zone-tailed Hawk. It apparently was attempting to drop in for a snack. I told the others to consider themselves lucky because the zonetail does not often afford observers such close-up looks.

When the excitement over the hawk died down, Wheeler's interest turned to hummingbirds. Two male blackchins and a male rubythroat had battled over the sugar water all morning. Wheeler decided to see how close to them he could get without spooking the hummers. First he stood ten feet away—still as a cypress. While the hummers continued to feed, Wheeler inched closer and closer until his nose touched the rim of the feeder. From less than four inches away he saw tongues flicking in and out to lap up nectar and gorgets magically turning from black to amethyst or ruby-red. He heard the whir of tiny wings and felt the rush of air as the hummers darted past his face. Wheeler held his finger near the perch, hoping a hummer would land on it instead of on the feeder. One hummer, hovering at the port, touched his finger ever so lightly with its diminutive feet, like a butterfly kissing a flower.

Wheeler had never been nose to beak with a living bird. He proclaimed this was the most awesome experience of his life. For a few magical moments my grandson, who was usually in perpetual motion at that age, stood still. The scene "through the one-inch picture frame" captivated both Kelsey and Wheeler, just as it had their grandparents all week. ᵰ

Through Juniper Boughs

In April, the show at Neal's goes on from daylight until dark. All spectators have orchestra seats. The script changes every few minutes as different actors appear. Some enter from stage right; others from stage left. Some have speaking parts; others are silent as mimes. Some creep slowly; others fairly explode onto the stage. Costumes are varied and colorful. Some of the performers make cameo appearances so brief that many in the audience miss seeing them altogether. Others are onstage long enough for the spectators to become well acquainted with them.

Evergreen boughs frame the proscenium arch. The small stage is tucked in among junipers and agaritas. The props are simple: a cedar log with holes drilled and filled with a mixture of peanut butter, lard, and corn meal; a sugar-water feeder; a plastic bowl with mealworms; a wire basket containing chunks of fruitcake; and sunflower seeds scattered on the ground. At midstage, water from a gallon jug drips slowly into a saucer four feet below, splashing over the river rocks inside it. Water droplets bouncing haphazardly provide the overture.

The show is about to begin one fine spring morning just as most of the spectators arrive. We take our seats and wait expectantly for the curtains to part. The background music is composed of a Canyon Wren's song cascading down the bluff, "cheer, cheer, cheer" from a Cardinal, the twisted notes of a White-eyed Vireo, and the loud jumbled phrases of a Long-billed Thrasher. Ever present and beneath it all are the drawn-out calls of dozens of White-winged Doves persistently asking, "Who cooks for you?" and warnings of "No hope!" from several dainty Inca Doves.

"Ooooooohs" and "ahhhhhhs" arise from the audience as a Hooded Oriole, dressed in an orange hood and black mask, comes to the sugar water for a sip of nectar. A Spotted Towhee—decked out in black hood, chestnut flanks, and a black cape with white spots—enters from the back, scratching through the seeds on the stage floor.

The bird with the rainbow on his back, a male Painted Bunting, enters and exits so quickly that most of the audience misses it. In the foreground, Ruby-crowned Kinglets, Blue-gray Gnatcatchers, and Wilson's and Nashville Warblers fly in, search for insects, and then depart. A White-eyed Vireo chases and catches a small yellow butterfly in its mouth, slinging it vigorously from side to side as if shaking a down pillow until feathers fly in all directions.

The fans are on the edge of their seats. Although enjoying the show, they still have not seen the stars that some of them traveled thousands of miles to see: the Black-capped Vireo and Golden-cheeked Warbler. Some spectators have come to the theater many times hoping to catch a glimpse of their award-winning acts. They know how lucky they will be even if all they catch is a brief glimpse of their command performances.

Suddenly, a hush falls over the audience as chattering notes fill the air. Soon, the actor wearing a dashing black cap and white goggles over fiery red eyes enters from stage left. He flits about between the water dish and the low-hanging juniper boughs before settling on the left rim of the dish. Just after he lands, a surprise visitor appears in the arena. A female black-cap lands on the birdbath from stage right. Everyone in the audience is breathless.

For the next few minutes, the two thespians put on a water show at center stage, enchanting the audience. First the male vireo flits into the water tail first, barely getting his feathers wet before flitting out and darting back to the branch. The female echoes his routine on the opposite side of the bowl as if choreographed asynchronously. The two water dancers repeat this sequence again and again. Their skit goes on for a full five minutes, every second of it recorded on videotape by Elbert Heath of Alpena, Michigan, who happened to be there with his camcorder.

The stars exit simultaneously. We wait for an encore, which never happens. This is the only time I have ever seen the male and female Black-capped Vireos at the water dish at the same time. Instead of bursting into applause, the audience leaves in stunned silence, knowing full well it has witnessed a once-in-a-lifetime scene in nature's never-ending drama. There are rave reviews for the stellar, show-stopping performance!

Then, just when I think it can't get any better than this, someone plops an extra cherry on my banana split. At least that's the way it seemed a week later, when a couple from England found a Golden-cheeked Warbler's nest behind the cabin where the water drip was set up. Even though I see goldencheeks almost every year at Neal's, so far as I know, this was the first nest found on the premises. The compact nest, located twenty-five to thirty feet above ground in the crotch of an oak tree, was well hidden by twigs and leaves. Finding it was a small miracle. So camouflaged is the nest, it's almost impossible to see it if there's no activity surrounding it. The day after the couple found it, the male and female goldencheeks came to the nest frequently to feed young. All was quiet the next day. No one knows for sure what happened. I like to believe the young fledged when we weren't looking.

Then, on a day in late April, I arrived at the "theater" early in the morning. My reserved seat in the orchestra section was exactly where I needed to be when the handsome, black-and-white bird with lemon-yellow cheeks (Golden-cheeked Warbler) entered from stage right. He landed on a low branch, looked around a few seconds, and then hopped to the ground near the dripping water. The audience held its collective breath as yet another award-winning performer stepped into the saucer, dipped his chest into the water and splashed it over his entire body. He then flew to a branch at stage left to preen. He flitted back and forth across the proscenium arch, making sure everyone in the audience saw him from all angles. We all felt as if several extra cherries had suddenly been added to our banana splits. ✒

Wandering Troubadours in the Texas Hill Country

I closed my eyes and imagined myself in a tropical rain forest. Hearing the array of squeaks, squawks, whistles, chattering clucks, bubbling notes, and lilting songs, I could easily have been in Costa Rica or Panama. Opening my eyes, I discovered I was not anywhere near Central America. I saw juniper branches still heavy with moisture from the shower the night before. Droplets of water, backlit by the sun peeping over the hill, clung to the green boughs like sparkling lights on a Christmas tree. Once again I was seated in the juniper bough "theater" in Concan.

As I sat before April's proscenium arch, there was no need to consult my playbill to determine who was who in the cast of characters. I knew the "squeaks, squawks, whistles, and chattering clucks" belonged to a Yellow-breasted Chat hidden somewhere in the thicket. The "bubbling notes" were from a Rufous-crowned Sparrow. He always sings offstage before entering. The "lilting songs" emanated from a Painted Bunting and a distant Canyon Wren.

From my front-row seat I finally spotted the chat singing (if you can call his weird sounds a song) from the top of an oak tree. I have never understood why the chat is classified as a warbler. It certainly does not warble. Nevertheless, *Icteria virens,* at seven and one-half inches, is the largest of the wood warblers. Its size, stout bill, and long, rounded tail defy its scientific classification, as most wood warblers are in the four-and-one-quarter- to five-and-three-quarter-inch range with thin, pointed bills. The Yellow-breasted Chat sports white spectacles and a bright yellow breast, so there was no doubt in my mind as to its identification. Most field guides describe the chat as shy and retiring. Consequently, I was surprised when he made an appearance at center stage. He was anything but shy when he boldly hopped into the water dish and began splashing water in all directions.

Yellow seemed to be the dominant color of the day. Soon a Common Yellowthroat with black mask and lemon-yellow underparts crept onto the scene. I don't know why it is called "common." It is an extraordinarily beautiful bird. Like the chat, this is another wood warbler without "warbler" in its name. It, too, went straight to the water, drank deeply, and then plunged in for a thorough washing.

The sight of a Yellow-throated Warbler almost always takes my breath away. The gray and white bird has a large white patch on each side of its head, black around the eyes, white wing bars, and a bright yellow upper breast and throat. Usually foraging high in the cypress trees along the Frio, the one I saw this day was in the junipers right before my eyes, completely oblivious to its audience. When it flew out in pursuit of an insect, it was so close I heard its bill snap when it caught a small white butterfly. In my opinion, the Yellow-throated Warbler and Golden-cheeked Warbler would finish neck and neck if there ever were a beauty contest for warblers. The goldencheek at the birdbath looked more like a painted prop than the real thing. Its black and white body provides a perfect foil for the stark yellow of its cheeks.

Other birds in the chorus line of yellow were Wilson's and Nashville Warblers. The Wilson's is olive on the back and yellow below, and the male has a jet-black cap. The yellow-bodied Nashville has distinctive white eye rings and a gray head. As if all that gold were not enough, as a finale, a Yellow Warbler in crisp new breeding plumage, yellow all over with red streaks below, suddenly appeared in an agarita shrub, looked around with its dark shoe-button eyes, hopped to the ground, and made a beeline for the water.

All this action could have taken place in a rain forest. The entire cast of characters spends its winter months in Central America, some as far away as Panama. I'm glad I had tickets for the spring performances of these wandering troubadours making their way through the Texas Hill Country. Who says there's no "gold in them thar hills"? ᎒

Bats, Comets, Eclipses, Nebulae, Cave Swallows, and Banana Pudding

What do bats, comets, eclipses, nebulae, Cave Swallows, and banana pudding have in common? Nothing really, but on April 3, 1996, something happened that linked these unlikely companions, causing a serendipitous evening. Four women from Kerrville, Medina, and Bandera, Texas, were participants in one of my customized tours out of Neal's in Concan. All day long we had explored one of my favorite birding hotspots, Park Chalk Bluff on the Nueces River northwest of Uvalde and wracked up a day's list of 80 species of birds. We arrived back at Neal's just in time to wash up for supper at Neal's Café and soon discovered the day's adventures were far from over.

"June, y'all better hurry and eat. The bats have been coming out pretty early, so if you tarry too long you may miss them." So said Rodger Roosa, our host and chef at Neal's. We gobbled down the fresh green salad, grilled chicken breast, rice and gravy, carrots, rolls, and honey that deserved much more time than we gave them. Belinda, our efficient and thoughtful waitress, packed our dessert to go. We invited my friends, Dwayne and Marj Longenbaugh, from Farmington, New Mexico, to join us for the outing.

We piled into the van and drove the five miles from Neal's to Annandale Ranch, where the historic Frio Bat Cave is located. After entering the gate of the ranch we still had two miles to go before reaching the cave. As we approached the hill in which the cave is located, I saw that Rodger was right. The bats, streaming out of the cave's front entrance, looked like a horizontal tornado. The main show had started without us. Many caves housing colonies of Mexican Free-tailed Bats also have large colonies of Cave Swallows, one of the most-wanted birds of birders who come to the

Texas Hill Country. Frio Cave is no exception. There's a twice-daily exchange of occupants in such a cave. Cave Swallows roost in the cave at night and feed during the day; the bats do just the opposite. You can see the swallow nests lining the walls just inside the cave entrance. It is a dramatic moment when the Cave Swallows swirl in the sky overhead, catching insects on the wing, before dropping like rocks into the top opening of the cave. When the bats decide it is time to exit for their night of insect hunting, they come storming out by the thousands. With their wings backlighted by the sun, the bats look like pen points of ink writing calligraphy onto the sky. From thick straight lines glistening in the sunset, they loop and curve into Os and Ls as if a great, unseen hand were holding the pen. The only noise you hear is the sound of the wind in their wings. They have been known to climb as high as ten thousand feet into the sky and are visible for up to two miles.

I have taken literally hundreds of people to this cave on dozens of spring evenings over the years, and the event never ceases to amaze me. Texas is visited by thirty-three species of bats every year. The Mexican Free-tailed Bat (*Tadarida brasiliensis*) is also called the Brazilian Free-tailed Bat. It is primarily a cave bat in Arizona, New Mexico, Oklahoma, and Texas. Approximately 17 million free-tails live in the Frio Cave from late February until early November. They live in Mexico and Central America the rest of the year. More than a million free-tails live under the Congress Avenue Bridge in Austin, making that group the largest urban bat colony in the world.

The free-tailed bat is easily recognized because at least one-third of its tail protrudes beyond the membrane that connects the legs and tail, hence the name freetail. These bats range over thousands of square miles each night. Bats are important to the environment because their preferred food includes moths and flying beetles—insects that are harmful to crops. Even though an adult freetail weighs only half an ounce, it consumes about half its weight in insects every night. Studies show that a million freetails can consume about fifteen tons of flying insects every summer night. To put this in better perspective, it would take nine eighteen-wheelers to haul off the equivalent weight of the nightly consumption of insects by 20 million freetails. Try to figure how many insects there are in a pound, and then try to imagine what the world would be like without bats.

But I digress. Shortly after we arrived among the whir of bat wings, the show suddenly stopped. I wasn't too worried, because sometimes the bats stop abruptly and then start out again after a short time. We decided to wait them out. After about thirty minutes, the bats again began to emerge. A Red-tailed Hawk, waiting offstage for the exodus, cruised over the columns of bats. Once in a while he attempted to nab one. Redtails usually catch their dinner easily, but this one seemed inexperienced and had no luck while we were watching. A Merlin did a quick flyby and caught a bat in short order.

Again, the emergence of bats stopped as abruptly as it had started. Thinking the extravaganza was over, I folded the legs of the tripod, placed the telescope in the back of the van, and told everyone it was time to go. Looking over my shoulder, I spotted the moon rising over the crest of the hill behind us. It was shaped like a half-eaten slice of watermelon, and at first we thought a cloud hid the top half. However, it turned out that the moon was in eclipse. Having been isolated from the outside world for several days, no one in our group had read or heard about an eclipse. What a sight! And what serendipity! We watched until the eclipse was complete. The next day, someone told us the best viewing was supposed to be in the East. We have news for them: Moon and Earth together put on a spectacular show in the Texas Hill Country.

Meanwhile, between views of the moon, we watched and listened to a Canyon Wren hopping around on the rocks, singing its delightful descending descant. We took turns looking through the scope at Comet Hyakutake. It looked like a blurry ball of light but was much more showy than Haley's Comet had been a few years before. We took long, lingering looks since another fifteen thousand years will pass before it comes around again.

Then along came another surprise. Dwayne asked if anyone was interested in seeing Orion's Nebulae. Of course, everyone was, so he focused his scope on that phenomenon. We were in a perfect spot for such heavenly viewing: far from city lights in a place where stars, planets, and comets look as if they are displayed on a black velvet cloth. We brought out the Styrofoam cups filled with banana pudding to celebrate the eventful evening, and everyone toasted the gods of nature. Then from a long distance came the bizarre call of a Common Poorwill: "Poor-will-ip.

Poor-will-ip. Poor-will-ip." We got back into the van to return to Neal's, declaring it a perfect ending to a perfect day.

So, what do bats, comets, eclipses, nebulae, Cave Swallows, and banana pudding have in common? Together they enlivened our senses of sight, sound, smell, and taste. They brought delight and wonder to an otherwise ordinary spring night in the Texas Hill Country for a bunch of awe-struck birders.

(The information about bats for this essay was obtained from Merlin D. Tuttle's *Neighborhood Bats,* and from two articles that appeared in *Texas Parks and Wildlife* magazine. One article, by Tuttle, was in the April, 1989, issue. The other, by Kelly B. Bryan, was in the June, 1992, issue.) §

Shutter Wide Open

I woke from a deep sleep to the loud jumbled phrases of a Long-billed Thrasher. Was I dreaming? Stretching and yawning, I tried to bring myself from the narcoleptic world of dreams to reality. The song of an Olive Sparrow like a ping-pong ball slowly bouncing to rest soon coaxed my warm feet out of my cozy cocoon to the cold tile floor. Half asleep, I shook my head, trying to remember—was I in the Rio Grande Valley where I had heard both songs many times before? No, I was in Concan, in the heart of the Texas Hill Country.

Our favorite cabin at Neal's shares the deck with the cabin next door, but we lucked out. No one occupied that cabin all during spring break that year. Harold and I had the place, the birds, and the stars all to ourselves. On this particular morning I knew the birds were waiting for me to replenish the seeds I had scattered on the deck the day before. Throwing on a robe and clogs, I shuffled to the front door, where I had stashed the birdseed. Opening the door as quietly as possible, I saw the Olive Sparrow on a low branch in a mountain laurel. I stood motionless in the doorway as the sparrow made its way to the sunflower seeds and raw peanuts.

The Long-billed Thrasher and Olive Sparrow are on a short list of specialty birds found in the United States only in Texas. Once I thought one must go to the Rio Grande Valley to find them. None of the field guides, except David Sibley's, affords the sparrow a range map, and his is not accurate. The books all state simply that the sparrow is found only in extreme south Texas. When I discovered Concan in 1986, I was surprised to find that the Olive Sparrow and Long-billed Thrasher are year-round residents there, far from "extreme south Texas."

Christopher Isherwood's words "I am like a camera with shutter wide open" played in my head over and over that week. My goal was to take photos of these two special birds. While Harold read murder mysteries, listened to classical music, and took naps, I sat in front of the bay window, camera on tripod, finger on the shutter release, relentlessly waiting for the birds to appear.

Waiting for the Olive Sparrow was like waiting to open the packages on Christmas morning. Sometimes it seemed the bird would never appear, but soon I discovered a pattern: First I would hear its distinctive song, then it would pop over the wall and begin scratching backward among the seeds with both feet. So, whenever I heard the ping-pong ball song, I would press my eye against the viewfinder and wait for the right moment to snap the shutter.

Olive Sparrows are usually solitary birds, spending most of their lives on the ground in dense thickets. Seeing them at my makeshift feeding station was a gift. I was surprised when two showed up at once. Since the sexes look alike, I assumed they were a "pair." The sparrow is soft olive on the back and tail with grayish-white underparts. It has bright pink legs, brown stripes on either side of its olive crown, a light lower mandible, and a white eye ring broken by a brown line through the eye.

When compared with the similar Brown Thrasher, the Long-billed Thrasher has a longer, decurved bill, a grayer head, and darker streaking on its undersides. Their ranges overlap only in the winter. The longbill is a year-round resident of the south Texas brush country. The Brown Thrasher ranges as far north as Canada during breeding season.

The Long-billed Thrasher's appearance on the deck was more predictable than the Olive Sparrow's. Almost twice the size of the sparrow at eleven and one-half inches, the thrasher stormed the scene like gangbusters. The smaller birds—House Finches, Northern Cardinals, Spotted Towhees, and various other sparrows—scattered when the thrasher appeared. It landed on the limb above the feeding area, and then went through the seeds like a vacuum cleaner, feeding so fast that it was hard for me to get its head in focus through the camera lens.

Spring migration was in full swing. While we were in Concan, White-eyed and Bell's Vireos returned for the nesting season. A local resident told us she had seen her first Scott's Oriole the week before. We heard a flock of Sandhill Cranes flying over one day heading north. We never did spot them among the layers of hills, but their distinctive trumpeting, rattling, "gar-oo-oo" call is a sure sign of spring migration.

Though we left Neal's only twice that entire week, we saw almost sixty bird species, most of them through the cabin's bay window. In nine days I snapped the shutter 132 times through that window and went home with five good shots of the thrasher and two of the sparrow. By week's end I felt I had become the "camera with shutter wide open." ❧

Silver Chalice

I am walking beside the Frio with one of my birding tour groups from Waco. Louise McCollum sees a tiny bird flit away and back to a spot on the lowest-hanging branch of a cypress tree. The bird's persistence in returning to the same location piques Louise's curiosity, and she points out the bird to me. The thin branch forms an upside down V, ten feet above the river's green water. From the bank where we stand, the spot is at eye level—making it easier for everyone in the group to focus on the right place. We see a small receptacle shaped like a miniature silver chalice attached to the limb at the apex of the fork. The nest, no bigger than a walnut, is a perfect piece of art. The Waco group discovers the nest on April 4. I return to the site often during the following weeks to observe the patient female hummer incubating two eggs. With my back to the rocky, wooded canyon wall I watch the nest from my folding chair.

The nest is in a young cypress at the edge of the river. Other cypress trees lining the banks of the Frio are centuries old. Their gnarled roots reach far out into the crystalline water. The new spring foliage on the cypress trees is bottle green. A gigantic boulder rests in the water next to the bank. The boulder has a row of southern maidenhair fern encircling the bottom like an emerald necklace. I feel as if I am in the Emerald City of Oz, where everything is in delicate tones of green.

According to Mayan legend, the birds that asked a tribal wise man how to build a sturdy nest were sent to the hummingbirds for lessons. And well they might have been. The architect of this fine structure is a female Black-chinned Hummingbird. She collects bits of plant down, weaving them tightly together and securing them with strands of spider silk. Through my camera lens I see the thin silvery threads that anchor the nest to the limb. After the inner chamber is complete, the little hummer gathers bits of lichen to attach to the outside walls with special glue, her own saliva, making the nest look like a knot on the limb. The finished structure is flexible and expands to allow for the rapid growth of two nestlings. Hummingbirds almost always lay two eggs, each about the size of a black-eyed pea.

By April 24 I see two tiny beaks above the nest's rim. The mother leaves often, returning a few minutes later each time. Perilously thrusting her needlelike bill deep into the newborns' tiny throats, she regurgitates nectar into their stomachs. I do not see any nectar-producing plants near the nest, so she must have to go a long way to feed. She occasionally makes quick forays for small insects to provide her babies with protein. Once, she returns with a small white butterfly in her bill.

After feeding her offspring, the female settles into the nest to brood the altricial young, who have no feathers and little down to keep them warm. The mother constantly moves her head and body from side to side, rocking the nest like a cradle. By May 5 the babies' bills have magically grown and appear as two rapiers pointing skyward above the nest's rim. As the mother approaches, both babies open their beaks, awaiting the food she pumps into their throats.

When I arrive the next day, the mother, perching above the nest, watches the nestlings as they take turns on the rim exercising their wings, which are now covered with tiny flight feathers. I predict "flight day" is not too far away. Sure enough, when I arrive at the nest site a day or two later, the nest is empty. Unfortunately, I was not aware that hummers usually fledge (fly) from the nest early in the morning. I simply arrived too late that day to see the special event for myself.

After fledging, young hummers never return to the nest to sleep or rest, but they stay near the site for about three weeks while the mother continues to feed them. After that, the female sees her offspring as competitors for food and acts aggressively toward them until they get the hint and depart to find their own feeding territory in another location.

It is hard for me to imagine that a bird as small as a hummingbird and barely a month old is ready to strike out on its own in the world of wildlings; much less that it will soon travel hundreds of miles on an uncharted path to a winter home it has never seen. Yet that is nature's way.

I never saw this family of hummers again. No matter how many words I read about nests and nesting behavior, I find there is magic in seeing for myself what really goes on around the nest. What an incredible reservoir of beauty and mystery there is in nature—and how much of it is all too easily missed! §♠

The Big Woods

The mostly sunny May Day was almost perfect, with temperatures in the sixties and seventies. A small group had just arrived at Neal's: six Hill Country women making their twelfth annual trek to Concan to search for birds with me. Having lived in this part of Texas most of their lives, these women know the butterflies, trees, mushrooms, endangered plants, and wildflowers of the area so well that I always learn much more from them than they do from me.

Bill and Patsy Cofer had given me a special invitation to take this group to a lovely place on their ranch near Concan. Annandale Ranch has been in the Cofer family for more than a hundred years, Bill being the fifth generation to own it. The Frio River runs through the middle of the ranch like a long, green silk scarf. The Cofer family affectionately calls this spot on the Frio the "Big Woods." It was a place I had never been before. They have installed permanent picnic tables and a volleyball net on the grassy area next to the river, giving family and friends a place to gather for picnics, fun, and games. My plan for this first day of the tour was to take our lunch to the Big Woods, which had never been visited by a group of birders.

The wildflowers were spectacular that spring. After entering the gate from the highway, we found that we were in a virtual sea of color composed of shades of yellow, orange, red, purple, and blue. We picked a colorful array of flowers. The winding, mile-long entry road led us from the locked gate, over the sea of flowers, into a tunnel of trees, and finally into what appeared to be the land of Narnia—the breathtakingly beautiful picnic spot. The Big Woods proved to be a magical place where we learned all over again the meaning of serendipity. The gigantic bald cypress trees seemed to reach their arms all the way to heaven, lending an air of reverence and dignity to the place.

Mealtimes with this special group are always sacred and ritualistic, a meaningful time of communion. After placing our flowers in purple vases, we set the two picnic tables with purple cloths, purple napkins, purple plates, and the purple vases.

I retrieved the CD player from the Suburban and started playing Bach. I don't know why. Given the elegance of the surroundings, it just seemed appropriate. Sharlande often reminds me that "at almost any time, someone, somewhere in the world is playing Bach." So we listened to Bach while getting the food on the table. I turned off the CD when we started eating so we could listen to the feathered symphony surrounding us with what seemed like digital sound. We heard the plaintive notes of an Eastern Wood-Pewee, the cheery tune of a Northern Cardinal, a Summer Tanager's robinlike song, a Yellow-throated Warbler's monotonous phrases, a Yellow-throated Vireo sounding like a sluggish Red-eyed Vireo, and the ever-delightful Carolina Wren's sprightly melody. All the time we were eating we kept a watchful eye on the river, hoping against hope for a Green Kingfisher to appear.

When we finished eating, I did something I normally don't do with a tour group. Since we were in virgin territory as far as birding was concerned, I played the Eastern Screech-Owl tape over my miniature amplifier to see what birds we could entice out of the woods. All the birds mentioned above plus a Black-crested Titmouse came to investigate the strange looking "owl" shaped like a black box. After a few minutes, one of the women heard an owl calling, but she said it did not sound at all like the owl on the tape. I turned off the tape player and listened. After a moment of silence, we heard the distant call of a Barred Owl, "Who-cooks-for-you? Who-cooks-for-YOU-awl?" Hearing that, I switched to the Barred Owl tape, and the owl answered, phrase for phrase. His calls became louder as he moved closer. Soon *Strix varia* was right over us. I focused the scope on an impressive, dark-eyed, twenty-one-inch owl of the river bottoms who was observing us as curiously as we were looking at him. He graced us with his presence for at least five minutes, giving everyone a chance to get an eye-to-eye look. He was so close that had he been blessed with eyelashes, we could have counted every single one of them through the scope. His curiosity about us satisfied, this denizen of the night lifted his silent wings and disappeared into the forest from which he had come. Needless to say, we were awestruck.

From Big Woods to Bach to Barred Owl, it was a mystical, magical, serendipitous encounter. Even though the group members had two more days to go on their tour, I told them they should go home right then, because I could never top that! §◄

The World Has Many Gifts

I fell for you "the first time ever I saw your face"—wrinkles, sags, and all. You were yelling at the top of your lungs, but I forgave you that. You had just been on a long, tough journey. I would have yelled, too, had I been through what you had.

You looked as if you had just come from a war zone. I quickly checked to see if all your fingers and toes were intact. They were. Opening your eyes, you seemed a little shell-shocked, as if wondering, "What have I gotten myself into?" Although I had never seen you before, I took you into my arms in a warm embrace and assured you that everything was going to be all right.

Looking deep into your eyes, I tried to discover who you were. Deciding that would take a long, long time, I introduced myself. "I'm your grandma," I whispered. "But I want you to understand from the beginning, I'm not your typical cookie-bakin' grandma. I won't be the one to teach you to make orange balls or fudge or date balls or the best way to cook a hot dog. I'll leave those things for your other granny. She has lots of other gifts she'll share with you, too. Why, she may even teach you to sing or play the piano or dance or do your multiplication tables."

Truth to tell, all of us—parents, grandparents, sister, brother, aunts, uncles, great aunts, and great uncles—have special gifts for you. Looking at the world with child eyes again, we're eager to see everything with you as if for the first time. I can't speak for the others, only for myself, when I tell you some of the gifts I want to give you.

The night we went to the hospital when your mommy knew for certain you were on your way, I saw a dandelion in our yard. Its fluffy head reminded me how much fun it is to puff and see little "parachutes" drift slowly to the ground. I can't wait to show you that. A dandelion head feels almost as soft as your skin. I want you to watch a nest with me and see the miracle of a baby bird hatching from an egg just as I watched your birthing and marveled at the miracle.

How old must you be the first time I show you my favorite places in Concan, dip your tiny toes in the Frio River, or christen you with its cold, cleansing water; place a smooth stone in your little hands and watch your long, slender fingers (so like your daddy Mike's) trace the outline of a heart; or teach you to listen with those exquisite ears (so like your mommy Catherine's) for the song of a Painted Bunting or a Black-capped Vireo?

I can't wait to hear your laughter the first time you see a jackrabbit scurrying across a field and I tell you, "It's named after you, Jackson Hayes!" I want to see your eyes light up when you see a hummingbird hover at a flower and watch its throat magically turn from black to ruby red or amethyst. I want to show you that a hummer's nest is so small it would fit into your tiny palm even now.

When you lie with me on a picnic table in Concan to watch for lightning bugs and shooting stars, I will teach you to find Orion's belt, the Seven Sisters, and Jupiter with its moons. Through my spotting scope I will show you the craters on the moon and the owl on the cliff as well as the scarlet and black feathers of a Vermilion Flycatcher. You probably won't believe me when I tell you a fuzzy caterpillar will soon be a beautiful butterfly. I will show you the tall cypress trees along the river and tell you that is the way trees pray: reaching for the sky, the moon, and stars. And I will pray that you live your life ever reaching for the moon and stars.

With Henri Nouwen, imagine that we could walk through our lives "always listening to a voice saying to us: 'I have a gift for you and can't wait for you to see it.'" Baby Jack, the world has many gifts. I can't wait for you to see them. ᏸᎇ

Benediction

Every April when I am at Neal's as the Resident Birder, I act as host to tour groups and individual birders. Almost daily I talk to scores of visitors—from England, Scotland, the Netherlands, Japan, France, Belgium, Germany, Australia, Bolivia, Canada, and throughout the United States—who travel to Concan to see the special birds of the area, mainly the Black-capped Vireo and Golden-cheeked Warbler. Inquisitive and anxious birders knock at my door at all hours of the day and night, inquiring where they might find certain birds.

One Sunday, instead of birders knocking at my door, I was awakened at 4 A.M. by loud rolling thunder and lightning like I have heard and seen only in the Texas Hill Country. The sound of rain hitting my tin roof and thunder echoing from hill to hill is a comforting sound to me, so I rolled over and slept through the storm. Hours later, when I awoke again, I still heard the rain, but the thunder and lightning had subsided. I knew there would be no searching for the blackcap or goldencheek this day, or any bird for that matter. I opened the door to check the temperature. The smell of breakfast from the café across the lawn sent me straight to my kitchen to cook eggs and bacon. I sat in front of the sliding-glass doors, eating breakfast while watching Olive Sparrows, Spotted Towhees, Painted and Indigo Buntings, and other birds feeding ravenously on the seeds scattered on my patio, and hummers and Hooded Orioles at the nectar feeder suspended from the rain-drenched tree.

It was a candlelight sort of day, dark and dreary outside, quiet and peaceful inside. This was a rare chance for me to have some privacy. I hung a "DO NOT DISTURB" sign on the door, lit candles, brewed a cup of chai tea, put a favorite CD ("On a Starry Night") in the player, and settled into a comfortable chair with journal and pen in hand. This was my idea of perfect tranquility. I placed a purple pottery pitcher filled with wildflowers next to the candles. Each exquisite design reminded me that God is in the details: a delicate yellow flax with a large dull-red spot lined with red veins extending up the length of orange petals; blue curls with flowers that look like little clusters of octopus tentacles; a two-petaled orange flower resembling a baby's bonnet; a purple goblet-shaped winecup. Seeing the candles and flowers reflected in the glass, it was as if I were outside looking in.

All morning, throughout the rainstorm, I felt as if I were eavesdropping on a steady stream of people going to the café—families, couples, and individuals. Some had umbrellas. Others did not mind getting wet. Soon I noticed a pattern: Before entering the café, almost everyone stopped to look over the stone wall at the Frio River far below. Most of the younger folks climbed onto the three-foot-high wall for a better look. One girl helped an older woman onto the wall. They stood in awe, side-by-side, taking a long look as if trying to memorize the scene.

The ritual of looking over the wall seemed to be a holy moment for each and every one of them, like genuflecting in front of the cross before sitting down for worship or saluting the flag in an act of deeply felt patriotism. Reading their body language, I tried to sense the way some of the people at the wall were feeling. Every time I stand in that same spot or at the top of the cliff overlooking the river canyon or sit by the river or watch a hummingbird at her nest or see a butterfly flit from flower to flower, I feel as if I am on holy ground.

Rain-lilies usually appear a few days after heavy rains, opening slowly around dusk, earlier on cloudy days, and expanding fully the next morning. Ordinarily, each flower lasts only a day. After the four-inch rain, rain-lilies sprouted everywhere. From a distance, some patches of the white flowers looked like blankets of snow.

One evening a few days later, a girl about eight years old began picking the rain-lilies that were scattered across the grassy lawn near my cabin. My first impulse was to run outside and yell, "No! Please don't pick them all!" But she was obviously in her own secret garden, so I remained silent. After the girl picked the last flower, she blithely skipped down the hill with the rain-lilies clutched in her hands, as if carrying a bridal bouquet. I hope she pressed one of them between the pages of a book. Then, when she is an old woman, she can take it out, turn it gently in her hand, and remember an evening filled with white flowers in the Texas Hill Country.

Like the little girl gathering rain-lilies, I have spent my life gathering memories—of birds I have seen and loved, conversations with birders I have met and shared time with along distant birding trails, of exotic places I visited in search of my most-wanted birds, slowly learning the wild-flowers of the Texas Hill Country, falling in love with rivers and butter-flies and trees and heart-shaped rocks. I shall tuck each memory into the corner of my heart where I keep such special treasures, and then, on some distant day, I will take them out one by one and recall the days when the birds, the people, the places, the wildflowers, the butterflies, the rocks and river beneath my feet, anchored my body and spirit in Holy the Firm. And in the beauty and peace of wild things and wild places, I'll be lost in communion, home at last.

Amen.

Epilogue

"The river is different every time I go there. I've seen it transformed overnight from a trickling stream to a raging torrent, its sides swelled beyond
belief, placid bottle-green turned to churning chocolate-brown."

I wrote those words in November, 2000. During the first week of July,
2002, devastating floods like no one in the area had ever seen before took
the Texas Hill Country by surprise. My heart broke into a thousand pieces
upon hearing of all the destruction dealt by this "500-year flood," as the
locals described it.

Damage reports on radio and images on television and in newspapers
made it hard to believe this was "just a flood," not a hurricane. Houses
that had been swept from their foundations careened down rivers like toy
boats a child might playfully have tossed into a stream. Cars, pickups,
barbecue grills, and long, twisted strips of metal from tin roofs ended up
in treetops. Centuries-old cypress trees snapped like dry twigs under the
force of the raging water, riding the current like tubers.

Bridges were washed away. Entire towns were cut off from surrounding areas. Someone saw a Great Blue Heron hitching a ride downriver on

a log. Ranchers were isolated for days, unable to get out; and no one could get in with supplies except by canoe or helicopter. Thousands fled their homes. I know these places. I know many of these people. I know the roads and bridges by heart.

Reading the *Waco Tribune-Herald* on July 5, I saw a picture of a bridge that had been partially washed away. I knew without reading the caption that it was the Highway 127 bridge over the Frio at Neal's in Concan, where I like to sit and watch birds as they bathe. I cross that bridge a dozen times a day every April. When I saw the cypress trees lying across the bridge, I knew one of them was the Black Phoebe's favorite perch where it guarded its nest and nestlings tucked *under* the bridge, supposedly out of harm's way.

Was the Black Phoebe in that tree when the forty-foot wall of water came crashing down, tearing it from its roots? There was no time for her to get her babies to safety. Nor was there anything homeowners could do when the angry, murky waters encroached on their property, inundating their homes, sweeping away many of their earthly possessions right before their eyes. And where was the Green Kingfisher? Surely all of its favorite perches had been swept away.

I was thankful that over the years I was able to memorize the Frio River, the rocks, the sky, the trees, the hills, the flowers, and the birds, because I knew in my heart of hearts that nothing would be the same when I returned.

On September 12, 2002, two months after the flood, I went back to Concan with fear and trepidation. I hardly recognized the place. Where stately cypress trees once lined the river, tons of river rocks now form a wide, expansive white beach. Around the huge boulder near which the Black-chinned Hummingbird nested, young cypress trees, snapped in two, now lean against the stone and each other for support. Gone is the necklace of maidenhair fern. Gone are some of the concrete picnic tables in the campground. Gone is all green vegetation in some areas. In short, gone is any semblance of the normalcy of former times.

Will it ever be the same again? No, not exactly. Can Mother Nature do a repair job and restore the natural beauty that all who go there have come to expect and love? Of course, but it will take time. And it will look different. In the meantime, I look for small surprises of beauty among the flood debris and see a tiny purple blossom sprouting beside a rock, rain-lilies in places where I have never seen them before, butterflies sipping nectar from miniature snapdragon vines, Cedar Sage still blooming in September when it was supposed to have stopped in July, the Black Phoebe perched on a stone in midriver instead of in the cypress that used to stand beside the bridge, a Green Kingfisher on a cypress stump, and thousands of new heart-shaped rocks washed downriver from heaven knows where.

Of course, it will be beautiful again: in the spring, when bottle-green adorns the cypress trees that stubbornly refused to give up their grip in the limestone riverbanks; in summer, when the river is flowing swiftly and tubers ride the whitewater all the way from one low-water crossing to another; in fall, when vibrant shades of red, orange, purple, and yellow shock you at every turn of the river; and in winter, when bare trees reveal their secrets of nests from which new life emerged last spring and will do so again next spring in spite of everything.

I know that new areas of beauty will spring up in the days to come, take me by surprise, and, yes, take my breath away. I pray that the remembrance of the Hill Country rivers—the way they *were*—will be the deep well from which the spirits of all those affected by this horrific flood can drink their sweet amen of peace. The flood of 2002 is one more reminder that out of destruction comes the resurrection of life, and that hope does, indeed, spring eternal. ❧

PUBLISHER'S ACKNOWLEDGMENT

The Texas A&M University Press is privileged to add its imprint to this Wardlaw Book. The designation claims a special place in the list of Texas A&M publications.

Supported with funds inspired by the initiative of Chester Kerr, former head of Yale University Press, this book, along with its companion volumes, perpetuates the association of Frank H. Wardlaw's name with a select group of titles appropriate to his reputation as man of letters, distinguished publisher, and founder of three university presses.

Donors of these funds represent a wide cross-section of Frank Wardlaw's admirers, including colleagues from scholarly presses throughout the country as well as those from other callings who recognize and applaud the many contributions that he has made to scholarship, literature, and publishing in his four decades of active service.

The Texas A&M University Press acknowledges with profound appreciation these donors.

Mr. Herbert S. Bailey, Jr.
Mr. Robert Barnes
Mr. W. Walker Cowen
Mr. Robert S. Davis
Mr. John Ervin, Jr.
Mr. William D. Fitch
Mr. August Frugé
Mr. David H. Gilbert
Mr. Kenneth Johnson
Mr. Chester Kerr
Mr. Robert T. King
Mr. Carl C. Krueger, Jr.
Mr. John H. Kyle

John and Sara Lindsey
Mrs. S. M. McAshan, Jr.
Mr. Kenneth E. Montague
Mr. Edward J. Mosher
Mrs. Florence Rosengren
Mr. Jack Schulman
Mr. C. B. Smith
Mr. Richard A. Smith
Mr. Stanley Sommers
Dr. Frank E. Vandiver
Ms. Maud E. Wilcox
Mr. John Williams

Their bounty has assured that Wardlaw Books will be a special source of instruction and entertainment to the reading public for many years to come.

ISBN 1-58544-292-5

90000